SOMEBODY'S
Always Hungry

ESSAYS ON MOTHERHOOD

Juliet Myfanwy Johnson

NELL BOOKS
an imprint of Wyatt-MacKenzie

Somebody's Always Hungry: Essays on motherhood
by Juliet Myfanwy Johnson

FIRST EDITION
ISBN: 978-1932279-92-4 hardcover
ISBN: 978-1932279-87-0 paperback

Library of Congress Control Number: 9781932279870

Essays previously published in the following:
Pete Fix It, published in *Los Angeles Family Magazine*
The Prison of Preschool, published in *The Foothills Paper, Los Angeles Family Magazine*
Old Yeller, My Pregnant Lungs, Dating the Preschool Parents, published in
    The Imperfect Parent
Birth of a Nathan, published in *Los Angeles Family Magazine* and *Cup of Comfort for Expectant Mothers*, anthology published by Adams Media
You Can't Take It With You, published in *MOMbo*; published in *The Foothill Paper*,
    published in *The Imperfect Parent*
He Rides Off, published in *MOMbo*
Pocket Dogs, published in *The Foothills Paper*
Free Lunch, published in *Mamazine*

NELL BOOKS
an imprint of Wyatt-MacKenzie

Wyatt-MacKenzie Publishing, Inc.,
Deadwood, OR
www.WyMacPublishing.com
(541) 964-3314

Acknowledgements

. . . .

Thanks to my family for being so supportive – Moose,
Grandandy, Gramma Susie, my brothers and sister,
Barry's family (all wonderful Oppers) and our friends
who have believed in my work; to Nancy for your visual eye
and business knowledge; to Chris for making
my words (and life) shiny.

Introduction

· · · · · · · · ·

Things No One Tells You About Having Babies

Here's what I'd do if I got pregnant again. Enjoy every moment of the transformation of the body. Don't worry about anything. On the way to the hospital: don't worry about what will happen during the labor and delivery. It's the one time in your life that you aren't in charge. You'll know what to do. If the pain is too much, you get the epidural. The epidural is great. It's like having a baby while standing at a cocktail party. Bring on the big contractions. It's just a bloop on the screen over there, behind the man with the hors d'ouevres. Then your doctor whisks in for the last seconds, you give three big pushes; the baby flops out; there's whooping, celebration; you feel confused, elated; a tiny stranger is put on your chest; you'll realize later you haven't lost any weight at all, and they wheel you to another room.

These two days are the best. Someone brings you food all the time. You don't have to get dressed. It is a little annoying that you can't sleep more than two hours at a time if you're breastfeeding, but like I said, people are bringing you food that you didn't have to make. And this is big. I'm five years in, with two kids, and there isn't an hour that doesn't involve some kind of food and me bringing it in. Having to buy food, freeze it, plan menus – the fun quotient is way down on the food. Maybe if I'd lived in the fifties, and worn one of those form-fitting Mom Frocks with the neatly belted waist and tasteful heels, hair and make up done, defrosting while singing a show tune I'd feel sexy.

The constant food production thing is the biggest change of all when having kids and staying home. And I don't have to actually bake the bread or milk the cow. No wonder pioneer women died at thirty-five. They died happily. They lined up to die.

In the hospital, there's a squirt bottle you use to rinse yourself off with after you go to the bathroom. Because nothing is going to touch you down there, not for awhile. You pack your underwear with ice. The underwear is really nice, too, it's netted and fits all shapes. And you are all shapes.

The breastfeeding is endless, and it's wonderful. It's a full-time job. The first time your boobs are useful. Your baby knows what he's doing and your boobs know what they're doing. You just sort of wrestle the six-to-nine pounder into position and doze.

They bring you all kinds of paperwork, you write the baby's name on a million forms. You start to worry that the baby's name is a stupid name. It looks so foreign. But it's too late now. I still worry about the name thing, though it's five years later, and my kids have grown into their names and beyond them. The name is a bookmark; it's something rather than calling them "hey you."

When you leave the hospital you aren't rested. But you've been celebrated, so you feel pretty good. Plus you've got the little bundle. In all those old pictures of my mom coming home from the hospital, or her mom coming home from the hospital with MY infant mom, they don't tell you that under those fifties and sixties dresses, their underwear is PACKED with ice. No one tells you what those flattering dresses are hiding. You can barely get out of the car. You're not in pain so much as awkward. It's the sheer amount of ice in your pants that is amazing. The ice is key at home, too, you want the ice. Helps for things like sitting down.

The first baby, I got out of bed every time I fed him during the night and sat on the couch to nurse, so as not to wake my husband. I changed his diaper, I cleaned him up. Second baby, I never got out of bed. She slept next to all of us —

husband, eighteen-month-old, me, and new baby. I just rolled onto my side to feed her lying in bed. Way easier. Who cares if no one else is sleeping. Because no one else is sleeping anyway.

Very important to have people in the house to make you food. The first few weeks especially. You're breastfeeding, you're starving, someone coming in with a sandwich is better than handfuls of cash. Bring on the mother or mother-in-law, someone to do the laundry and make food.

The first shower you get, that first ten minutes alone with the baby in the other room, is like winning a trip to Hawaii. The water feels like Paris itself. The shower is the only place those first few months where I felt human, not like a glob of Momhood.

Things you'll need: Get the simplest car seat. You'll switch to a booster at three years old for the next three years. The infant seat thing will only last about a year. Get a light weight stroller. The simplest. You'll need a nursing bra, you'll need the lanolin nipple cream. That saves you from getting chapped skin.

Then for the next two years ignore everything you read, everything people tell you. Trust your guts. Don't stop nursing your baby 'til you're ready. Don't give up sleeping with her in bed if it makes you happy. Don't give away your time with them. Even though you feel like you're going crazy from your life slamming from sixty to zero in those three pushes during labor. Stay at zero. It's quiet like no other time in your life. Watch bad television. Let yourself live under a blanket with that baby. You won't regret it.

It helps to have a great lover in your life. Someone who recognizes how important your job is, and who loves kids, and is in love with life. You will be looking to this person as the eyes and ears of the outside world, and you need that close friend to talk you off the ledge, or help you understand what you're going through.

I didn't really wake up for about a year after having my first baby. Then we had another baby, so I was out for another year and a half. When my oldest was four and started preschool, that was a huge shock. Suddenly society was intruding into my own little private haven with my little boy and baby girl. I resented it incredibly. Sure, he needed to socialize, but why don't they tell you that the warranty is only good for three years on a baby before they have to enter society? Suddenly we had to be somewhere, at a certain time, three times a week. I ignored people and only went twice a week for six months. I wanted my time with my boy. I didn't make kids to foist them off on other people, even though I want to throw them through a wall sometimes. (That's something no one ever tells you either. You get MAD. I was never a yeller or an angry person 'til I had kids. Now, man, I can YELL. But that's covered in a later story.)

Your rhythm will completely change. First, you'll be astounded. Then as you get used to caring for the baby, your rhythm becomes their rhythm. And if you just go with it and try not to go crazy, the rhythm will start to feel really comfortable. It's a much slower pace. You have to stop and look at lots of things. Nathan is almost five and was writing his name on his birthday invitations tonight and he wrote "N – A –" and then said "Oh, look, an ant," and I looked next to his card at the ant on the table. Then he finished writing his name. Everything has meaning. It's all happening, right in the moment, and that kind of living – living while looking around you – it's impossible and exciting. There's ALWAYS something going on to look at and investigate, and be scared of, or be thrilled by. Planes going by. Trucks backing up. Coyotes howling. Bees in the pool. People walking by to greet. Things to tow behind the tricycle. Popsicles to eat.

The summer before kindergarten, all the other preschool moms and dads were worried about having their kids home all summer. There was the great Send Them to Camp rush. But I had had enough of hurrying to get them dressed in the morning. By June, I was ready for the break. I boldly said no to camp. The first day of summer we stayed in our pajamas all day. Emma, Nathan, and I got up whenever we wanted, and proceeded to climb in my big bed – or wait, we never got out of our big bed since we all sleep there – and we watched television as long as we wanted. Then we went swimming. Then we had lunch. Then we took a nap. Then we went swimming. Then we took a walk. Then we had dinner. Then we read books. Then we played a game. Then we took a bath. Then we got ready for bed.

We did a version of that pretty much all summer. There was the beach and some movies, but for the most part, the summer hit us like a cozy out-of-town gramma with flabby boobs. We were in her embrace, and she fed us lemon drops.

Enjoy the exhaustion. Enjoy the anger. Enjoy the far off look you get from your husband when he's trying to place who you are. Enjoy the never having a moment off. Leap in. Lather it on. Celebrate your life. Be where you are and don't rinse.

Table of Contents

· · · · · · · · · ·

Introduction

Things No One Tells You About Having Babies 7

Little Babies

My Pregnant Lungs 18

Birth of a Nathan 21

Baby Rabbit Hiding 25

Pete Fix It 32

Baby Fashion 35

Pocket Dogs 40

One, Two, Now Three 44

Preschoolers

The Prison of Preschool 50

Is This Your Turtle? 57

You Can't Take It With You 60

Old Yeller 65

Dating the Preschool Parents 70

The Tortoise and the Hare 77

Ski School, or Here, Carry More Stuff 85

He Rides Off 93

Elementary School

The Practice of Leaving 98

Home Cooking 101

Learning to Swim from a Three-Year-old 106

The Family Bed, or You'll Never Go to the
     Movies at Night Again 108

Dead Bunnies are Easier to Carry 112

Paul Small 116

The Cat People 118

Nathan Sleeps With a Severed Arm 122

Santa Can I Have That? 125

She's Beauty, Now 129

Free Lunch 135

Silkworms 140

Chain of Fools 144

The Cheese Stands Alone 153

The Tooth Fairy is Coming 156

I'm Done 160

Walking in Puddles 165

Epilogue

Saving the Bess for Last 172

About the Author 181

Little Babies

My Pregnant Lungs

I've gotten to know my lungs pretty personally in this last, ninth, month. Before pregnancy I really had no relationship with my lungs. But since the baby has pushed his feet into the North end of what had always been lung-occupied territory, the lungs are tapping on my lower esophagus, trying to catch the freight elevator up to someplace – anyplace – in order to find some breathing room. In the last few days I've thought, "What if I suffocate from the inside?" I've been suffocating from the outside for years now, so the feeling wasn't different, just inverted. What if the baby takes up more room in me than <u>I'm</u> using?

Lungs are like very serious substitute teachers. The ones that come in with their own assignments for class, not the ones that let you read or sleep all period. Lungs slap on the chains and climb the mountain road in the snow if they have to, starving, if they have to. They hate the baby. They barely tolerate exercise, but they definitely always counted on having their space. In their natural state, the lungs are a comfortable yuppie gay couple living in a spacious loft apartment in SoHo, and this baby is a three hundred pound redneck cousin who has come to visit. Naturally, they're devastated.

The baby stomach in general feels like you swallowed a

backpack and it's strapped on in front of your spine, filled with water balloons. The baby is hanging there, one foot planted in each lung, swinging and dangling, and the lungs are trying like hell to stay attached to the ribcage.

Lungs are a lot lower in the chest than I thought they were, too. The way I breathe, if I had to guess, I'd say my lungs were located somewhere in the sides of my neck. With pregnancy, you can locate your lungs easily. They're pulled way down, like gramma's sagging boobs, almost halfway to your belly button. Apparently, the lungs run into your back, but in this case, all the pieces have come forward and lined up for this baby emergency. They're working as a unit, lining the flooded street with sandbags, ordering soggy sandwiches, boarding up windows – anything to help stave the impending onslaught.

When my body reaches maximum capacity, in those last few pregnant seconds, I hope my lungs heave a monsoon breath and shoot the baby out like a loaded spring – then, the gaping silence. There'll be the baby, over there, everyone crowding to see him. My body will be rearranging itself in the aftermath, like the end of a Tom Cruise war movie. My lungs will be staring around at the rubble – breathing again, pulling a tattered shirt over a scraped shoulder, alien defeated, walking home, breathing deeply, victoriously. In a perfect scenario, months later the memory is gone, my lungs are flat shelves, guys that work in an air conditioned office with plenty of vacation time, wondering what all the commotion was about.

Birth of a Nathan

The baby shocked me out of myself. Lying in the bed with the nurse, Patty, I had met hours ago now seated between my legs on a spinny stool, cheering me on like the coach sister I never had, all these months of waiting and harboring the inner seven pound beast and he snakes out of me silently, like a breath of frozen air. There he is, blue, wrapped loosely in the cord, the newly appeared on-call doctor that I've never met (fresh and gay though he has no idea and has gotten married) holds the baby up and hands him over to me, up on my stomach, and I can't remember this part, this seeing the baby. The nurses are scurrying around rattling pots and pans like they're preparing for a church picnic in the 1840's, and the man, the Dad, Barry, is on my right and he's breathless and confused, and there's this baby – this wonder mint, this tiny dot of skin, of stillness, of wonder, a blank silent cupcake of love on my left – and I can't catch my brain or my heart; they've gone. There are no words for this part. You think there might be words, or at least a special noise or a color, but there's nothing but a tiny little boy and – wasn't there supposed to be a girl? But here he is and gone I am, and there is only love.

He's always in motion – arms going in circles, legs going in circles. Impossible to believe I grew that in my stomach, that something so perfect came from someone like me. There must be a God because I would've forgotten something important. The bridge of the nose. I would've skimped on that. It would've been a drawbridge.

They take the baby to warm him up and they roll me and my dead legs onto another bed to take me to a room. It's all surreal because I just spent nine tedious months waiting for the wonder of my life, and then in ten minutes he's born. He just slips right out, like he's been waiting in line at a buffet, and he's just paid, and then people are using his name and I'm wondering "Is that a good name?" and they're weighing him and footprinting him, and his screams sound like carnival music and then they wheel me to the other room and I'm put in a bed and given mesh underwear and my stomach feels like a bean bag, gentle and soft. I keep putting my hands on it in wonder and kneading it, feeling it pliable and loving it – my body, the transformation of body.

Everything is going to my breasts – words, milk, love, humor, family, meals, dogs, fights, all of it turns into milky liquid and the baby eats. I have no free hands, nothing frivolous to do with my hands like before, no time for wiping my eyes, a leisurely scratching of the nose perhaps. The baby brings loss right to my fingertips, he has not taken all my time, he has freed my time, he celebrates my body. He uses me. He cries. He knows exactly what he wants, and it's me, he's sure of it.

The hospital is safe. It's always night, because I'm always in my pajamas, and the shades are drawn and nothing bad ever happens. People come in to tell me various things about my boobs or my bottom half, my family comes in and out, and I can only tell because I hear my mom's high, lilting laugh and I am stapled in with its safety. Nathan and I live like bats in the ceiling of a church – hanging upside down, filled with blood and catching all the faith floating up from below on music.

The nurses surge over us in gentle six hour waves, *Here's medicine, Here's food, Are you all right?, Isn't he beautiful?,* and the sunlight comes and goes and Nathan stays. Nathan's here now. I write his name on a million forms and I like the shape of his letters, the repetition of the sounds, the way he begins and ends the same way.

It's three a.m. and he's lying in the plastic hospital bassinet beside the bed – a tiny white mouse I feed all the time, and the light from the bathroom yellows the room into a brown duskness. I change my pads, and wear the netted underwear, and stare at my son, and stare at my son and I can't believe the swirling of the earth around my head.

It's still night and Barry and I stare at the baby we made, sleeping, no bigger than a pile of spent birthday candles. We look at him because there's nothing else we can do – we're helpless; we're trapped in his sonar, his love grip, and we stare at his little breathing form and sort of glance at each other sideways because it's so packed with emotion it's hard to make eye contact without exploding or disintegrating. We can't believe we're here. Certainly still in the infancy of us, and here we are with this brand new life in a hospital room in Florida, in steamy hot August.

I get scared of being a mom, of not being able to do it and Barry tells me, at three a.m., in his quiet way, "You just have a new friend, that's all," and then he smiles at me.

With the birth I see that everything Barry's been telling me for years is true – that you do everything from your heart. Your brain makes a lot of noise and tries to run things, but you put everything on a shelf and do it from your heart and you wait and you get things like the birth of a Nathan. Even though everything outside of the little pale plastic hospital bassinet holding Nathan in is falling apart, there is hope in the room. Barry keeps coming in and out of my vision, and I can't understand how we've made it this far, and I can't look too closely at the enormity of it all. Like when I saw the Grand Canyon. You can only focus on the first hundred feet, the rest is a painting.

Baby Rabbit Hiding

I let the eleven-month-old Emma drive over to Junie's house. Two-year-old Nathan stands on the passenger's seat with his head out the window, blond curls plastered down by one mile per hour wind (the baby is a cautious driver on our quiet back neighborhood street).

We decided we needed to see Junie after spotting her across the (cement) L.A. one inch river that runs between our houses. Her adopted horse George, and adopted goat Diana, had gazed at us lazily from the side yard while Nathan yelled an unintelligible hello.

Junie's house is at a dead-end next to a huge empty field. We do a U-turn and park messily. When we get out, we see the white basket on the porch, and three little gray kitten heads pop out like fake twenty-five cent Chinatown toys.

"Awww, look honey," I say, holding the baby and "helping" Nathan out of the car by hefting him by one armpit and setting his bare feet down on gravelly cement. I wonder if I should've gotten him shoes when later it'll be more important that I've forgotten his diaper.

"Titties?" he says, looking for the cats, his blonde head craning. "Baby 'eyows'?" he says earnestly and lets me hold his hand across the overgrown, thick and wild lawn. Careful not to trample the white baby's breath flowers.

On her door is the snowman wreath, three green wreaths stacked up like a snowman with a scarf around his neck that is still hanging there, a remnant of Christmas a month earlier. A Christmas bone. Like our Christmas tree laying abandoned in our yard, on its side, where our land-lord has recently come and hacked it to bits with a chainsaw. Dante and his chainsaw.

"Hi kitties," I say, eager to see them even though I am allergic and don't particularly like cats. But little things, all little things, are worth a moment to stoop down and watch.

"Be right there," our neighbor's voice drifts out from behind the snowman, and Nathan and I sit on the porch while a few kittens tumble out of the basket. One heads directly for the old food lying out. I set the baby Emma down a step, but she climbs back up slowly, shrieking, point-ing at the cats with bright eyes and saying "DAH!"

Two yellow rain boots lay discarded on the walk a few feet from each other, on their sides like dead soldiers. Children's boots, from one of Junie's two adopted school-age kids, Grace and Albert. Her whole life is adopted. The horse. The goat. The five dogs out back. The seven kittens in the basket. And all of them have names from the royal family. Victoria. Elizabeth. George. Charles. Veronica. Diego. Okay maybe not all. But a real tendency.

"Hiii...," our neighbor says shyly, sliding out on the porch, not meeting our eyes, moving like water around an oily molehill. Junie creeps everywhere. When we first met she told me she was incredibly shy, but it isn't just shy, it's distant. Something or someone had made her blank. What had happened that could erase someone so effectively?

She's a gentle height, her fair hair back out of her eyes casually but exquisitely, I notice, at every time of day. Her clothes are powdery and appealing; she is attractive, soft, and yet there is something untouched. She looks like when no one is around she probably floats to things.

She manages to sit down without taking up any space. "Hi guys," she says softly to the kittens. "Anyone wanna come out?" She talks to them from across the grass while we sit on the porch near them. I think of how barbaric I am with animals. You take them to the grass. You PUT them there. You don't address them from far away. I discreetly begin unloading the kittens one by one – we'd be here for hours if we had to wait and see if they'd come out.

Nathan ignores the cats in the basket and looks at the cat food. "Mommy?" He points at it. "Poo poo?"

"No poo poo, honey."

Emma has climbed down the stairs and is eating dirt.

"As long as there're no rocks," I half-joke.

"No, no, it's good –" Junie pauses, eyes trailing off. "Minerals."

We watch the kitties attack each other. I peek at her. Her light green overalls don't have any stains on them. Her wispy nature almost allows you to see directly through her.

"They have such a human cry," she says suddenly. "When one is lost in the house, I hear her cry and I say 'I'm right here!' and I hear the kitty say 'Where?' The tone –" she pauses, "The inflection…is mine. Like mine. Because their mom died, I think. They sound more human." Three cats have crawled up her legs. One sits in a dump truck toy.

"Mommy, nooo…." Nathan points at the kitty in the toy.

"You want to play with the toy?"

"Yeahhhhh," he whines.

"Go get the kitty out, babe," I say.

He goes forward and takes the cat out by the head.

I think about his new game. When he doesn't want to go to sleep he snuggles up under my arm, shoving his head under till it's hidden and says, muffled, "Baby rabbit hiding."

"It's a new game," his dad had said to me the night before. "Before he wanted only that book, only to see the piggies crying or the pickles and now no – 'Not that page, Daddy. New page', he tells me. And where did he get this 'baby rabbit hiding'?"

The tail I pinned to Nathan's sweats before we left home lies smashed under his butt as he plays with the truck. Still hanging on. I cut the sleeves off a fleecy baby shirt I was giving to Goodwill, stuffed the sleeves inside each other, got a diaper pin, fixed it to his butt, and made a tail. He's been obsessed with tails lately. 'Beeeg' tails. And 'babee' tails. I see her looking at it.

"He had to have a tail," I explain.

"I noticed it. When he came up." Her voice trails off vaguely, although her interest is genuine. She's like tepid tea in a mostly empty restaurant, while you're waiting for someone who's never gonna show up.

"I like this little white one," I say, of the little boy kitty that had the cutest face.

"Yeahhh…." She looks thoughtfully at the sidewalk, a gazing daisy. "After you left last time, he looked after you, followed you. He said to me, 'Am I supposed to go with her?'"

She pauses. "I talk… you know. I'm an animal communicator," she says suddenly. Long pause. "I don't know if you know that."

I know laughter is wrong. Feel like laughing.

"Ohhh," I say, trying to be open-minded. I mean, who knows, this is L.A.

"Yeahhhhh." She doesn't really go into it and I don't really ask fearing the answers. Plus I have a psychotic older brother who constantly phones me from Washington state saying he's met Jim Morrison up there and he's arranging for his comeback. It just feels too similar. I really want to wait for the movie on both counts. Grab a cab ride back to reality.

"I wish we could have a cat. But I'm allergic."

"Me too. Not deathly."

Somehow her words come out silently while mine sound like conversation. There are acres of quiet. I grab my bigger baby for ballast.

"We have to go soon honey."

"Noooo," he whines, just because. Truthfully he's been bored of the kitties as soon as he realized there was no fresh poop to investigate.

Months ago, out on our stroller walks, we started bringing apples to Junie's horse George, and got to pet all her various animals, which is what started our relationship. When we first brought apples to George, she told me she was almost forty. And she had pretty much given up on the idea of romantic love. There had been nobody she had really loved. She was considering marrying our landlord, Dante, who had proposed to her half-jokingly over the trash cans he was pulling in one day. Dante with the chainsaw. He can hardly hear. He's seventy-four. He's probably proposed to the trashcans themselves at some point.

"Okay, punk," I say to Nathan, hauling myself in my old sweatshirt and hospital pants, and ugly too-big brown shoes of my husband's, manhandling the smaller baby while wiping dirt off her happy chin with the waistband of my sweatshirt.

"You can ride up front."

"No, bahck," he says insistently.

"There's a stroller in the back. Front, with the window down."

"Vindow? Down?" He looks at me, impressed.

"Thanks Junie," I say as we start across her lawn.

"Oh no problem," she still crouched on the grass, under cats. Almost in a ball.

Nathan curls his blonde head under my arm.

Baby rabbit hiding, I think, watching her.

Pete Fix It

When the fax machine breaks, and Daddy is steaming, three-year-old Nathan takes a look at it and says, "It's okay. Take it Pete's. Pete fix it."

Pete's the mechanic. Barry's car recently broke down and we went to drop it off at Pete's. On the way to the garage, Nathan picks up his play phone. "Hi Pete. Daddy's car comin. Has hole in tire. You fixin it for us. I in me's tractor, I just be in me's tractor all day. Bye."

We get to Pete's place, a sea of hurt automobiles. My tiny blonde babies walk the strip of steps in front of the building. Pete's meeting us there. He's out with his wife. Nathan is silent watching for Pete. He cannot speak in anticipation of Pete, the greatness of Pete, who can fix anything.

Pete shows up in a Lexus, a gleaming silver new SUV. There is a beautiful lady in the front seat – long dark hair, gentle smile. She waves at my kids.

Nathan looks at her like a sailor looking longingly out at an empty ocean. Almost two-year-old Emma waves at her. Nathan forgets all about Pete.

"Who that lady?"

"I don't know, honey."

Pete talks to Barry about his car. Nathan studies Pete's wife while Emma rubs her hands around on the asphalt and looks thrilled with her black fingers.

"Her nice lady?"

"She looks nice."

"Her not bite?"

"No, she doesn't bite."

"Mean people bite. Mean people pinch too."

"You're right. It's better not to do that."

"Her not do that."

"I think that's Pete's wife."

He looks at me like I just said she was Pete's toaster oven.

"They have kids. That's the mommy. Pete's the daddy."

"Oh."

We leave the car with Pete.

Outside, at home, Nathan gets out all his "tools me got from me's birsday" and shows Emma and me how to "fix" the plants "like Pete." How to fix the dirt. Make it into soup, chicken. Animal tracks. Taste it. "It not too hot." He's in his thick training underwear, the cozy looking white ones with thick panels, long legs shooting out the bottom, lean, strong brown tummy and flailing arms shooting out the top. On top of all that the talking Nathan with his white curls soft as a silent movie star. He sees the dog, Maisie, and runs after her, abandoning us in the dirt with our shovels.

Emma sits on my lap and we pretend to pick the

embroidered cherries off her dress and eat them. We've eaten almost her whole dress when Nathan reappears with his doctor's badge on and pretend scissors in his hand. "Just givin Maisie hair cut." I look at Maisie's guilt. She was enjoying the attention. He brushes Maisie with my brush. "I brush you's hair too, Mommy. Me doctor." Emma offers him a pretend cherry from her dress. He accepts her offer, but at the second one says "No moy. No thanks Emma." He is using a tongue depressor to brush my hair.

"Me three. Me big. Me two yesterday."

"You're three now, yep."

"What happen two?"

"Two? You used to be two."

"Me like two."

"I like two too."

"Where two go, Mommy?"

"Well….It's behind you now."

He looks over his shoulder.

He pokes my eyes with his pretend scissors and Emma gets into the act, brushing my hair with the hard end of the brush, dancing in place excitedly for no reason. What happened to two?

Pete, fix it.

Baby Fashion

We are scheduled for a nine a.m. fitting at Baby Gap for the Baby Gap fashion show. Fitting today, show on Saturday. We'd been coerced into this highly idiotic entry level of Show Business while buying baby socks with a gift certificate, the only way I can afford to shop at Baby Gap.

Since we are awake so early, like every morning, awake before any living human being should be conscious, I take them to the park to kill time before beginning their fantastic foray into short-lived modeling careers. It's so early all the slides still have that mysterious night-water on them. We play and I nostalgically look for that E.R. chick that I saw there last time and who made me feel in touch with the famous people. Finally, we'd have something to talk about. But alas. Apparently it's too early for famous people to be up, too.

We run to the mall late for our fitting, and this lovely gay gentleman, Victor, who sports casual clothes (slightly wrinkled striped shirt, shorts), and a lisp that seems medical and not feigned; on break from UC Berkeley or some UC perhaps UCL Gay, anyway, he's very sweet, and gets down to Nathan's level (who is very into playing 'dress up') and helps him choose an outfit. I steer them away from those acid wash-bleached-stripe-down-the-front-stupid-ass jeans that everyone is wearing now, and fifteen minutes from now, and to the more classic jean instead (size 3), which Nathan wears with a red zip-up jacket over a white oxford long sleeve (their fall line). He tops it with a red hat with a truck on it and a sports bag bearing the GAP label, which he is most excited about. Not the label, but the bag, any bag, every bag. As I write there are three bags strewn about, the last one he packed had a bowl and a tennis ball in it.

Back to fashion – I have the baby on my back in the backpack, which she loves, and I keep ramming her into displays and knocking stuff off racks as I spin around looking at Nathan's various clothing opportunities and choices.

We have to change in the bathroom while Victor shops solo for the perfect outfit for Emma, so I help Nathan get dressed, which is hard enough one time in a morning and certainly not what I was hoping for when we were assigned this fitting. I thought maybe I'd be sipping tea with the ladies and discussing the Italian Renaissance while someone else dressed and played with the children, parading them by when they were ready so we could throw them some change or mini-muffins, which they could scrounge around for on the floor like urchins.

The only other mom there is a Greek lady who has a pile of clothes and is trying them all on her baby, whom I think is named "Mental" or something, I can't catch the name. And all Mental wants to do is lay on the floor with her shirt off. Who could blame her? They ARE really nice floors. Smooth, polished, hard wood. My kids just stare at Mental with dazed looks on their faces, assuming that Mental knows what dress up is all about since we have never been to dress up, and have only rushed through the Baby Gap together at lightning speed to return something. (The prices being too scary for us to dawdle.)

In the bathroom, Nathan needs no help ripping off his rainbow shorts that a very pregnant chick at the park earlier called 'girly' clothes — since when did rainbows become strictly girly? — and jamming on his jeans with his sandals still on. Then I silently curse Victor (or "that guy" as Nathan is calling him) because I have to button up a very long Oxford shirt which means bending over with Emma on my back and heaving her forward and almost into the toilet. Victor knocks softly and offers us Emma's outfit — a pink dress, white sweater, and puffy white hat.

I wrestle her out of the backpack while Nathan checks the toilet to see if it "flush all be itself" which he's been fascinated with since we saw the self-flushers at Disneyland — and I take off Emma's overalls but — tired already — leave her shirt on and jam her, shirt and all, into her little pink dress, buttoning the (price tag, $69) sweater (laughingly because we would never buy a $69 dollar sweater unless we could all sleep under it or drive it), and put on her fluffy white beret and then we are ready.

Nathan waddles out of the bathroom now dressed like a forty-year-old frat boy, saying "Where that guy?" I tell him we have to show the guy what we are wearing so he can keep them for the fashion show. Nathan is *very* concerned that Emma have a little bag to carry too. "Just like me's," he says. I'm just hoping Emma won't pass out from the three layers of clothes she now has on, in August. She's quiet through the whole thing – she takes her dress up very seriously, apparently. She has her serious lips on.

When Victor and the other sixteen-year-old who's working come over, they realize another kid will be modeling Nathan's jacket, so they get Nathan a blue jacket and hat (which is much better), and Victor (at Nathan's reminder) grabs Emma a little white purse which she LOVES.

Then they stand there so Victor can take a picture, but his camera isn't working, so he runs to the back, and that's when my kids are staring at Mental lying on the floor while her mom berates her from beneath a big pile of clothes in the corner.

Victor never gets the camera to work, so we just have to go back to the bathroom, undress, redress in 'street clothes,' hang everything back up, then take them out to Victor, who saves them for us. I have to fill out questionnaires that ask questions like what're Nathan and Emma's favorite color, animal, superhero, etc. – very tough when kids love everything, and everything is their favorite, because that's how life is. It's all good, especially what's happening at the very moment you ask, unless it's naptime or a bee sting. (I realize later that the questionnaire is what they read when they walk down the runway at the fashion show. Which is too bad because most of my answers are "Teletubbies.")

Nathan's very excited about the dress up experience this Saturday. Too bad it's at eight-thirty in the morning.

Afterwards, we rush over to meet Poppa and Aunt Linda and the cousins at this EAT place that we go in Los Feliz, and Nathan drips most of his chocolate milkshake all over his shirt happily, licking the bench if it dripped onto that, while Emma stuffs eggs, potatoes, pancakes, tuna, and pickles into her mouth, and then goes to hang on the fence. By some weird coincidence, Daddy/Barry is there meeting with someone about a small movie he's hoping to produce, and we say hi but can't eat with him, so in the car after we leave, Nathan says, "That sad Daddy not goed with us." And I say, "Yeah, it's sad when we like to be with Daddy and he's busy. But what's good is that we'll get to see him later." Then he promptly falls asleep.

In his rainbow shorts.

Pocket Dogs

The kids and I dash across town and make it to library story time in time to run to the bathroom first. Three-year-old Nathan wants to try his new skill of going pee-pee in the stall next to me while I go in the giant handicapped stall to give the baby room to pull toilet paper apart and spread it around the floor, which will distract her long enough for me to pee before she looks down and remembers she can crawl under the stall door, her newest and happiest discovery. I sit on the toilet seat not realizing until I stand up that it's completed soaked my butt. I go to the sink, holding the baby and watching Nathan to make sure he doesn't stand too close to the bathroom door and get hit, which he's managed to do every time we go to the doctor's office. I doubly hope no one comes in as I balance the baby on one arm, and shove paper into my pants to try and clean up whatever wet toilet pee was on me. I try to think positively. I'm strong, I can take a little pee. Must remember to throw pants away once at home.

At story time (which is packed with every flavor of sweating human), Nathan climbs down to sit on the floor with Ziani, his tiny cousin, who comes late with her mother, and then Emma has to climb down to sit with them, leaving a wall of people between me and them. I sense disaster, but decide to remain hopeful. They sit for a full twenty seconds, in the front row, inches in front of the librarian dude who happily reads a book about dogs-in-a-pocket to the group. Everyone's blissful and attentive. It's just like <u>The Sound of Music</u>. I feel strangely relaxed for one fat moment.

Then Emma leans her head to one side, crawls to the librarian's foot and lays flat on the floor on her back like a beached starfish. Nathan leaps to lie on top of her, and you know, tries to smother her with love, or just smother her and this large woman in front of me looks back at me like *Bad Mother.*

I squeeze through the crowd and drag them off each other. Emma, happy to see me after such a long absence, grabs at my purse, and when I try to take it from her I can see she's going to scream her lungs out, so I let her hold it as she tries to wrestle the bubble gum out of it which she's not allowed to have, and Nathan, when I grab his hand to pull him over so we're not DIRECTLY IN FRONT OF EVERY-ONE, falls limp like he's been shot with a tranquilizer dart. My instinct is to drag him from the room, but there is EVERYONE staring at me like a Greek chorus-jury, and the librarian is reading and reading, and it's all sounding stretched like he's at the end of a cartoon tunnel, so I pick up Emma, who is dangling the purse and screaming now, and crouch down and pull Nathan while trying to appear healthy and well-rounded, and the librarian keeps reading "Pocket

Dogs" like it's the best book ever, as we edge backwards to the wall and sit where we can't see the book at all. And this is our story time.

I don't know why I try to do the crafts. This week it's pocket dogs, like the book, where you glue a paper dog into a pocket of construction paper. I always do the craft alone while Nathan tries to cut up everything, or glue the paper to the table. Emma wanders to the window where she can sit in the sun, gaze at the people below and take all the paperbacks off the spinny shelf and strew them around on the floor. I watch little cousin Ziani and her mom glue everything on carefully and perfectly, with laughter and discussion

Leaving the library is the best part. Taking the stairs down, climbing the stairs back up, going down them again; it's like a holiday. No one is staring. Nothing is damaged. There's no screaming.

Once at home, I'm trying the new naptime-put-them-to-bed-crying-thing, which is sucking. It's supposed to be good in a few days. Sucking right now. I'm thinking of abandoning it. And while I go from one room to the other to 'comfort' the hysterical children, I hear the puppy, Owen, throwing up under the table in the kitchen. I clean that up between bouts of hysteria.

Once they're both asleep, I lay on the bed surrounded by our library stuff, a pair of hiking boots, and a bowl of wet paper towels. I think about my house being a wreck and all the boxes of old toys I can't throw away, and when was the last time I had a conversation with my husband that had big words in it? And what happened to my friends? And didn't I go to college? I think about Emma's eyes getting wide when she slaps my chest in the middle of the night to tell me "WADDO" which is her word for water, and her demanding gesture at the night stand. I think about Nathan on the way home from the library saying, "Sleep me, mommy." And even though I feel dry, sucked dry, cracked, caked in baby, it's a lush tropical dry, like the green grass in flat hot Palm Springs. There is a stabbing sense of good in loving my babies, in their flailing, fast-paced, intricate lives, in my juggling and exhaustion to keep up with them, every day, every night. "Sleep me, mommy," says the tiny voice from his car seat, his angel white curls on top of his sleepy face.

My husband wanders by on his way back to his home office. He looks in at me, at my decrepit, limp body on the bed. "Good day?" He says, hopefully.

I hold up my construction paper masterpiece. "Pocket dogs."

One, Two, Now Three

Sunday is Nathan's third birthday party and I work my huge fingers to the bone. (Everything about me is huge. I ate cake yesterday – and okay, some for breakfast, but it is really good cake.)

It's a hot day, which is good because at least we're outside with very little shade. All of Barry's family is there…I say all like thousands of Jews crossed the desert…. There are the Little People (Barry's nieces, all hovering around five feet tall), and their tiny spawn, there is the patriarch Old Poppa (who brings Nathan a bike and a can of cashews). There's the college brother, Bruce, who shows up with hair as long as the girl who comes with him. That fashion of wearing your jeans hanging almost to your knees with your underwear out is still hot, apparently. And my Valley family, director Dad and Stepmom, my skinny sister with her fiancé. And my mom who lives next door but is the last one there, pushing her huge wheelbarrow of The Past and offering out pieces to whomever stops to talk to her.

Birthdays, when they're your baby's and not your own, are like a death-clock counting down. We watched a tape of Nathan at birth, at one and at two, and he makes these big changes; it's like a joke, the time speeding by while you're working your ass off with barely a breath. Nathan's this little blonde timepiece, racing across the lawn, curls bouncing, naked. One, Two, now Three. I know there'll be a time when he won't be naked, a time when he'll dye his hair purple maybe, a time when he'll wear his pants like they're falling off his ass like Bruce, and I suppose I'll be shocked then, too, at how fast it's going.

These baby years are *hard.* It's so *detailed*, and intricate, like you're constantly defusing a bomb – sweating, fingers in tiny spaces, unhooking minuscule wires, hoping not to blow something sky high. And that's just the living room. Then you go to make lunch. Another rewiring. Then bathtime. Then all the times in between. "Find me's nogs" (his clogs) "Find me's ha-has" (Binaca – when you breathe out to test your breath you go "HAAA HAAA.") "Where's me's tool kit?" and every time the question and his face looking up at me like "Don't fail me, Mom. I'm hanging on the edge of a cliff here. I've GOT TO HAVE THAT TOOL KIT. AND WHERE'S ME'S OTHER FWOPPY SHOE?" It's ALL EXTREMELY IMPORTANT.

I know it'd be easier to be a mom who doesn't know, all the time, exactly WHERE the other floppy shoe is. It'd be so much easier to just wear adult clothes and go to work each day. In my car, alone, in the sunny yawning silence.

This challenge of doing it all right, and doing it all well, and paying attention to things, loving them, showing up, being there….I'm tired! Soul tired! My life is all shredded, my body's a wasteland, and my heart is huge, bloated, full, blood-red worn, but I think motherhood gives you a bigger ache, the ache to do well, to care, to succeed. When Nathan looks up and needs something, I want to succeed. Not just because or if he cries. But because I can do better.

We started decorating for the party the night before. Barry went to get stuff at the store. The guy is good. Not good as in to look good, that's my specialty. Barry's good because it's RIGHT. Under all his own junk, he's a pure soul. Under my own junk, I am more junk, and then under that pile, there's a tunnel, and then a rock and under that is a room where the doors are locked, but if you break a window and crawl on your stomach you find a little jewelry box, and if you open that, under the little cotton square you lift out is a tarnished ring, and if you open the front of the tiny ring you find a tinier speck of dust, and on that is my soul.

We're evenly matched.

Nathan is very excited about his party. Emma wants to wear his underpants and clothes to the party. I have to move her clothes out where she can reach them. She can only reach his shelves.

Then it's happening. People show up and suddenly I'm on fast forward. It's hot, I'm running around, can't find the camera, there's food, kids in the pond, presents opening. The pinata is made of IRON, will NOT break, and Uncle Robinson keeps holding it over the tree limb by a string, a Marine, looking hungover and strained. I finally cut it open violently, with scissors, and then all the kids rip into the candy. Even though there's only three kids and two babies it seems like a hundred, and then it turns out later they leave their candy bags by accident so now I have a crapload of bubble gum and Smarties.

We go inside to eat cake since it's now ninety-nine degrees outside. Of course someone turned off the air conditioning so we turn it on but meanwhile I can feel sweat running down the sides of my body and if I'M hot, I know my Dad's broiling, but he's next to me doling out ice cream like my hired goon, God bless him. I'm most proud of my Teletubbies on the cake that I made out of food coloring and icing, they turned out so well I took a picture.

We eat cake and Nathan sits on Bruce's lap next to the cake, so, on the corner of the cake nearest to Nathan, all the icing is scratched off with finger marks.

Then suddenly it's time to go and everyone is leaving, crowding around me, and then the yard gets cleaned up and the house gets vacuumed, and the kids get washed and go to bed, and I lay on the bed with my head near the foot, which is how I sleep when it's hot, and Emma lays spread eagle, and how fat do I feel? When breastfeeding stops completely (I'm down to once a day, at closing time), I'm hoping I can watch those pounds go down the drain.

And, truth? Watching those videotapes of baby Nathan, and even six-month-old Emma, the silent suddenly sister, seeing three years condensed into ten minutes of videotape, seeing Barry and I looking like normal, happy people, seeing the kids shrieking, growing up happy, dogs and dirt and ice cream, our house slowly filling up with too many toys…. It's a big hearty life. There is no truth separate from it. I am living crowded, loud, jumbled. I may never sort it all out. I am piled beneath it, frail, and in awe of it.

Preschoolers

• • • • • • • • •

The Prison of Preschool

At preschool today, they are making magic mirrors. Four-year-old Nathan is having none of this activity stuff.

"Look at the glue. Look at the glitter! You can put on beads!"

The bead table is one of three tables inside the little stone building that has sucked my son's babyhood right from me like a high powered vacuum. Well, not all of his babyhood. He's still enjoying anxiety and fear.

He looks at me with big eyes. "I want you stay, Mommy."

"I know you do, but I have to go."

The panic in his eyes starts to swell.

"Stay 'til I do all the tables. Just 'til I do all the tables."

Two-year-old Emma is squiggling at my hip. She wants DOWN. She wants to go to school NOW. She would trample Nathan to get to those tables.

All the way to school in the car, all five blocks to the school, Nathan starts his fear. "I don't wanna go to school."

"Why not?"

"I don't like my teachers."

"Why don't you like your teachers?"

"I don't know."

"Your friend Michael will be there."

"Stay with me, Mommy."

I make a glue circle on the magic mirror. Glue, normally the ultimate glory to have in his hands apart from real scissors, and he's not interested. He's staring at the giant fear cloud that is forming around him. Making him impenetrable by teachers and other tiny people. Nathan has started to Shut Down.

Emma has wriggled down and is making her own magic mirror, having stolen it from a Chinese kid, and wields the glue and glitter bowl like a pastry chef.

I kneel down and help Nathan pick out beads, talking about everything in an upbeat way like the books say, trying not to look at him too deeply, but he stares at me like he's facing a firing squad. He's disintegrating.

The happy sound of kids playing turns into a wave of sickening background noise. The trees and park setting around his little preschool have turned into a ghastly knoll. Nathan grows silent and begins to suck all the air and the space from between us until he is actually under the skin of my leg and winding up me like a third artery.

"Honey. Michael is here." I point out the huge five-year-old, solid as a truck stop, coloring a magic castle.

Nathan's vision has gone. The room is black. The teacher leans to talk to him but her voice has become an evil, hoarse sputter. He is overwhelmed by the breath, her ogre stench. Michael is an hallucination, a distant memory of someone he killed time with while in prison once. Oh yeah, Monday. Two days ago. The prison of preschool.

He's glued one bead onto his mirror, by accident. One hand clutches my pink dress. I gently try to loosen the grip, getting down to his level, catching one of his petrified eyes with mine.

"I don't want you to go."

"I always come back."

Tears start in his eyes.

"Go to the park," he tries, desperately. The park right next to the school. If Emma and I go the park he spends the first hour of preschool yelling out at us every three minutes, "HI MOMMY!" I have to give him his own life.

"Just go to the park," he says. I scoop up Emma who is having none of my scooping. The teacher writes Emma's name on the back of her magic mirror. Emma runs over and lies across the castle drawing table.

I can't get Nathan's fist off my dress. "Mommy. I don't want you to go."

He's full-out crying now. His face sweaty, and terrified.

"I want my handkerchief!"

Oh no, we have forgotten the handkerchief.

"I'll get you a tissue."

I cross the room. My heart is in my shoes, sloshing as I

walk, the heaviness of Nathan's fear tangling in my attempt to be a good mother.

The tissue box is gone.

"Oh, we're out of tissues," one teacher notices.

I am for a moment paralyzed. *There must be some hanky replacement.*

"Let me get a paper towel," the older teacher says, the one I can never read to see if she hates me and my child who cries every time, though we've been coming for six weeks in the summer to get used to preschool for the fall, so the fall will be easier. The fall is two weeks away and it's not getting easier.

"I need a hug. Mommy. ONE HUG. Mommy. Let me kiss you." He holds up his arms, frail as a drying starfish. His tears on my face, his hot little lips, all the blood goes to his lips when he cries. I HATE PRESCHOOL, I think. THIS IS BARBARIC.

"Here, Nathan, have you made your castle yet?" the teacher is trying to guide him to the table. He's hysterical now. "MOMMY! ONE MORE HUG! MOMMY!" He gives me more wet and desperate kisses and hugs. I pull the plug on Emma's good time and try to head out of the room looking strong.

"MOMMY!" He calls to me.

I haul Emma to my hip, certain now that he'll hate me for taking Emma from this hell but leaving him, like <u>Sophie's</u>

<u>Choice</u>.

"I'll be back! I love you, honey!" I look back at him, corralled by the teacher, wrestling with her, crowding his friend Michael; he's red, crying on everything, holding his arms up, eyes full of fear.

He sees he's trapped, and cries out suddenly: "BYE BYE MOMMY," his voice breaking, his attempt to be brave cracking out of his three foot frame. His bravery breaks my heart in half.

I leave out the front door.

Emma looks at my face. Usually she says, impressed, "You not cry today, Mommy!" But today she is silent.

The park is flat and vast, the trees shoot up around us like giant stork legs. Everything looks white. The air has gotten wider. Why do I pay for this school? Why can't he just stay home and grow old and uneducated in my attic? That feeling of leaving someone who doesn't want to be left – it's cruel. Doing it twice, three times a week. It's killing me, the walking away.

I get in the car. Emma plays with the windows while I collect myself. He's so little. He was practically just born. That birthing class we went to, out in the country. Where all the women either worked at the prison, or had been there, as clients. Then he slipped out, he was only the size of a meatloaf. *How am I ever going to do college?*

For four years we did everything together. I saw everything that Nathan saw. I could picture what he was thinking, I was part of his experience. I know he's not mine, he's made of me but he's purely him. I just didn't want to find out so soon. *This motherhood thing is a scam. You get four years in and there's no way you're getting out, because your heart is gone. Your heart belongs to the boy.* So you have to do the right thing.

Emma and I do errands together, alone, for three hours.

We go back to pick him up at school. He's in the swarm of kids running outside from tree to tree, running back to the teacher, like on the mountains in <u>The Sound of Music</u>. He doesn't see us. He looks up at his teacher the way the other kids look up at the teacher. He's happy. He tilts his head back like he's taking a shower in a waterfall. He glistens, but that's because he's mine.

He sees us. He leaps over and climbs into my arms and wraps his legs around me. He buries his head on my shoulder. So happy, he has no words. I'm a tree, and he's my moss.

We walk to the car with his magic mirror.

"How was school? Did you have fun?"

"Yes."

"Did you play with Michael?"

"Yes. I made Daniel a friend."

"You made a new friend!"

"But he doesn't share. So I might not make him my

friend."

"Did you sit on the steps at lunch?"

"Yeah. All the little kids sit on the steps."

"So, see, school is fun. You always don't want to go and then you always have a great time." I seat belt him in.

Nathan looks longer, like he's grown up from the bottom of a lake, made of thick mud. I can see his frail hold on life, his four year grasp. His face looking up at that teacher in the trees. Hope, there's hope.

"I don't want to go back." He says, happily.

Is This Your Turtle?

I've almost gotten Emma to sleep at naptime. It's one-thirty, I've been trying for an hour. She's blinking slowly. Her breathing getting regular. The doorbell rings. Twice. Really loudly. She pops awake.

I get out of bed, cursing my mother because I'm sure that it's the UPS guy in his slick brown outfit, d e l i v e r i n g yet another one of her purchases from late night T.V. – perhaps another bracelet, a lamp, or some shiny baubles – I open the door, and there's this Asian gardener dude standing there with his arm up holding something and he says "IS THIS YOUR TURTLE?"

I stare, in wonder, at this beautiful sentence. "...No."

He shrugs, and walks off.

I close the door and go back to Emma, getting back in bed. I lie there feeling funny, like my skin is made of bubbles. It's so nice to have something – surprise me.
I'll probably never in my life hear that sentence asked of me again – there are some things you get once in a lifetime, and I could feel this was my one time.

I look at Emma. "Don't get out of bed," I tell her. I get up, go back out the front door, see the Asian dude and his Mexican cronies starting to pull out from the neighbor's driveway in their van. I walk over to them. I lean in their window, like we're old friends.

"Hey. Where's that turtle?"

"Right here." One of the guys holds it up. "You want it?"

(Ummm)"...I want my son to see it."

"Take it," the Asian guy says. "We have too many animals."

One of his cronies hands the turtle out through the window.

"We have too many, too," I say.

The guy waves me off.

I head back inside. Emma is pretending to hide under the sheets when I get back to the bedroom. "Hey, Emma, look." She unburies herself. Sees the turtle. Her face can't register it, like I have an elephant on my palm. "Where did you get THAT?"

In the last twenty-four hours, the turtle (actually a tortoise) has now: been to the movies, ridden on a tricycle, played in the sandbox, been in the hammock, been zipped in a bag and taken on a horseback ride in Griffith Park, been pushed on the swing, been towed behind the bike in a little four wheeled cart lined with hay.

If the tortoise could talk, he would whisper "I HATE YOU."

In the car, with the tortoise between them, here's the conversation:

N: The tortoise loves me more than he loves you.

E: (indignant) NNNOO!

N: He does.

E: He does not!

ME: THE TORTOISE LOVES YOU BOTH THE SAME.

He's sleeping by the bed. His name is Winky Grass. Turns out he is our turtle.

You Can't Take It With You

"Can I take this to school today?"

Nathan has a purple beach bucket loaded with a flashlight, a Sponge Bob wallet stuffed with fake money and old credit cards, three rocks and some crackers. This is how it started. First it was crying at school. Now he wants to take everything with him.

The first day he took a bale of hay that he conned his gramma into buying for him at the art supply store. Kid size, it was only two dollars. He will not unwrap it from its original plastic covering. He put it in a Ralph's plastic grocery bag for double protection.

As we get ready for school, he's toting the miniature hay. Daddy keeps pointing at it over his coffee, going, "HEY! HAY! HEY!" while we all stare at him until we get it. As we leave to go out the door, Nathan is still holding the hay.

"Honey – what're you doing?"

"I just want to take this. Can I take this hay?" His big orphan eyes.

"What do you need it for at school? You want to show your friends?"

"I just want to take it. Just this. Nothing else."

We've recently started a new rule – No New Things in

the Car. Started because we could no longer see the floor of my car, the kids climbing in and out over a sea of dolls, toys, shoes, candy wrappers, books, lunchboxes, Kleenex, old cups, and broken sunglasses. And that's just the top layer. We haven't seen Nathan's best friend Karina for awhile, but I'm hoping for the best.

Every time I wash the car we fill three garbage bags with junk, and the bags sit in the living room for weeks. In the car there's a breath of blue, a hint of a void. There's so much free space that for several hours we can think of having another baby, or even getting a bunny.

Then a doll appears. A pair of socks. The legs of a toy. Badminton rackets. A deflated basketball. Old lollipops. Golf tees. It's autumn in my car, and the kids are shedding new stuff each day.

"Only ONE thing in the car," I amend my new rule, and my husband shakes his head. Nathan has had such anxiety at school. Taking a bale of hay isn't going to hurt anything.

At school he puts it in his cubby. I look at all the other kids' cubbies. Dora backpacks. Princess lunchboxes. Spiderman sweatshirts. My son – hay bale.

There's something great about requiring the unnecessary. It twists a new coil in the brain, turns a light on in a dark place, somewhere up in your head, to have a son who values hay bales over backpacks. It isn't the thing he values as much as the valuing of something, relishing the specialness of some novel new object.

Too soon life fills with the necessary – the wallet, the proper clothes, the right change, straight thinking, the steps to the top, success, achievement, purpose. This is his time to float. Nathan shows me the value of focusing on the *one thing* at the moment that brings you joy. And then taking that thing (preferably in a plastic bag) everywhere you go.

The next day I'm holding Emma, the two-year-old, under one arm in her pajama top with milk smeared all over her face, rushing to get us out the door to Nathan's school on time. I block Nathan with one foot at the door.

"Wait, what's that?"

"What?"

He's holding a beaded leather notebook and an old soapdish in a Ziplock bag.

"What's that?"

"I'm taking it to school."

"You don't have to take something every day," I say.

"You're taking something," he says, looking at Emma.

The next morning the pool man comes early because something has been sucked into our pool filter. He's about eighty years old and it's not looking good for the pool, or the man on wet, slippery cement. Nathan stands somberly at the diving board, taking in the fix-it activities very seriously. I'm yelling to the pool guy that I'll be right back, chasing Nathan to get him out the door. He clutches two rolls of paper towels, one under each arm like a wrestler. Looks up at me with big eyes. "Can I take these," he says, urgently.

The next day it's his red play tool kit. Inside are some magnets, a hammer, and a piece of cheese.

The next day, a roll of tape inside a trash can. I have to draw the line, some line, any line.

"You can't take that with you," I say.

"I can," he says, assuredly.

"You can't take everything with you."

As the floor of my car fills up once again, and I am living the end of <u>Titanic</u>, all the stuff floating up up up until we drown or jump, Nathan brings "just one more thing" to school. A pumpkin. The little plastic table from the middle of a pizza box. A piece of black plastic pipe. Two dolls in a Tupperware bed with cloth diaper blanket. A roll of adding machine tape fastened with a yellow paper clip. A tiny rake and two shovels in an eyeglass case.

For awhile he couldn't go to sleep unless the Tupperware bed was next to him. Now it's the tiny gardening tools next to his pillow in their eyeglass case. "Babies can pway with them," he tells me very seriously at naptime, and I look at his tiny teeth. "Not the rake. But the shobels. They're not showp."

He found his treasures at Half-Price Wednesday at the

thrift store. He put them in an eyeglass case. He looked at all the other eyeglass cases, sitting on the floor, opening them, looking up at me with an earnestness. One had dark blue velvet on the inside.

"Mommy, you want this one? It's soft inside." His big, blue plush heart shone out at me. I love that he can find treasures on the floor of a run down thrift store, that he feels rich with the choices, his life a bright stream where the oddest throwaways have possibility and light.

As I make meal after endless meal, watch <u>Mary Poppins</u> for the thousandth time, or take another trek to the cultural mecca that is my grocery store, I think about Nathan and his bags of treasures. As I haul the kids in and out of carseats and brush their teeth and pull on tiny pants and tie shoes and answer questions like "Who invented food?" and watch them fall asleep and see their live faces and silent fingers, I think I know what Nathan is talking about.

He stands at the door, four years old, wearing my striped tights and holding a fishbowl filled with marbles.

I'm taking it all with me.

Old Yeller

In my twenties, there were days – maybe weeks – that went by where I never spoke much or even raised my voice. I had the comforting presence of a twelve-year-old girl walking quietly to church to sing in the choir.

Now I am this:

DON'T TAKE YOUR CLOTHES OFF!

DON'T HOLD THE DOG BY THE LIPS!

LET'S NOT THROW DIRT!

DON'T SQUEEZE HIS NECK!

DON'T EAT GLASS!

The police action of being a parent is the biggest drag. You have to police everything, or they'd be constantly scraping the paint off the wall with screwdrivers. And my kids are relatively calm. My husband is better at handling all of that than me, because he relayed an important and true fact to me early on – everything bad that they do, it goes in phases. The biting might be really bad and scary right now, but next week, it's magically gone. It's quick.

"YOU MAY NOT HURT ANOTHER PERSON!!"

"WHY DID YOU PUNCH HER??"

"WHERE DID YOU PUT THE PENNY?"

"SHE WANTS HER PENNY BACK!"

"WHY DID YOU DO THAT??"

"WHAT IS THE MATTER?!"

"WHAT'S GOING ON??"

I'm constantly yelling like a blind person being ignored at a loud party. I can never be ahead of the danger; I'm always slightly downstream from it, hearing the yelling escalating, trying to throw or wave my hat to get someone's attention.

Here's what I realized: no one is listening to me. I'm yelling because no one cares at all what I'm saying. I'm the necessary white noise in the background. I'm the T.V. turned up really loud with just static playing. The kids are still having their fight. In the car: "She's looking out my window! Tell her to stop *looking!*" Me yelling, "STOP YELLING!!" We're in traffic on the freeway; there's no exit out of this life that can come soon enough. I realize I'm going to be having these enjoyable yelling intervals not just for today until dinner time but FOREVER.

I am powerless. I can't stop my mom from reading me the ingredients off a soup label first thing in the morning when I stagger out to make the kids cereal and she's been up all night as a night nurse, and she's telling me why each individual ingredient is important. I can't stop the hole in the ozone layer. I can't even get my kids to stop fighting for *two minutes.* Even with the yelling. Then I remember I never listened to my mother either as a kid. I never thought about my mom always yelling from the other room. Her anger was humorous, and not very interesting. My brothers and I would be having our battles over toys or food or the spot on the couch, or what to watch on T.V. , not thinking that the noise my mom was making in the kitchen had anything to do with us. Then suddenly she'd be looming over us, face severe, yelling something but none of us could really hear any of the words, we were so struck by the comic look of her anger. Jeez, what's SHE so mad about?? I see that look on my kids' faces when I come in the bathroom and rip the squirting toy out of five-year-old Nathan's hand that he's been using to spray soapy water directly into Emma's eyes for the last ten minutes despite her screaming, DON'T DO THAT NATHAN!! I come in and RIIIIIP, take the toy, yelling, the kids looking thrilled with this drama, watching me with wonder, and an ounce of pity, and then they're happily playing again, for two more minutes, until the next disaster.

There's futility there. The futility is that there IS no hope for this and every police action, except for protecting the injured party and constantly establishing and reestablishing rules. They aren't going to remember the yelling; they don't remember it a moment later. The yelling is reliable, like leaves falling in October. You count on it, but it doesn't MEAN anything. Its presence just reaffirms for the kids that they aren't living in a void. The mother duck will always come in and reherd the ducklings. It's a louder kind of herding.

Also, when I yell, it makes Nathan yell, because he does-n't like getting yelled at either. Then we're both yelling, and making mean faces, and you can't laugh because then they'd KNOW I don't REALLY care if he runs after bunnies in the petting zoo, or throws his sweater around glass ornaments in a tiny shop, or spits soda at the wall outside, or climbs on my car. (Get off my car. GET OFF THE CAR! DID YOU HEAR ME??) Then there'd be NO rules, and there have to be rules or we'd be having candy for breakfast while painting direct-ly on the furniture, and dialing so many random numbers on the phone we'd finally connect overseas. The fireplace would be filled with gasoline and matches, scissors would be lying around everywhere next to permanent markers, and they'd be cutting up money and licking quarters. The fish would be drowning in handfuls of fish food, dirt and rocks would coat the bottom of the swimming pool, the bathwater would be ice cold, dirt would be the new shampoo and the Shrek soundtrack would be blaring. Wait a minute, things wouldn't be all that different.

The kids don't realize that I'm the only one working this party. They run the racetrack I've put down for them, and it's a good run, that's why there's so much free time for this glorious boundary testing and the emotional joy ride I get of having to directly face my light side and my dark side, alter-nately, every minute of the day.

I'll be glad to move on from this stage. I'd like to return Old Yeller to his former glory – a love story about a country boy growing up with his gentle yellow dog who suddenly goes rabid, and then there's crying and a gun and tragedy looming in the background. But I loved the movie. It's the love story that sticks with you.

Dating the Preschool Parents

I wanted Nathan to have friends. All the other preschool moms and dads looked so professional and relaxed. Then there's me, at the mercy of my four-year-old. Whomever he likes, I must like, and Nathan would do anything to have Michael play with him. His version of trying to play with Michael is to stand next to me in the classroom and hold my leg. But I know how desperate he is. So if it's Michael's friendship he wants, here I go.

I stay at school when I drop Nathan off, and try to stand casually, in close proximity to Michael's dad, Scott, the stay-at-home kind. Michael's dad laughs nervously. We have a little chit chat, like we're in a bar in college, and instead of drunk coeds it's tiny tables filled with glitter and scissors, and everyone is under three feet tall.

Michael's dad reminds me of my first boyfriend, Thomas. Huge. Probably rode a motorcycle at one time. Still awkward around girls, and we're both pushing forty. It's not really that cute. It's cute that I'M awkward. I'm a girl. He is holding a baby, which helps. As I scoop some conversation out and apply it to his skin, I can see that we're not meshing. I'm meshing. He's out of the mesh.

Luckily Michael is in love with me. He has no friends either. He's only five. I have to *initiate* asking Scott out to the zoo with Michael "sometime," his eyes not meeting mine for very long, giving a nervous laugh, then a "Yeah, that'd be great," and me saying "I can get us in for free, I have that pass." Then him saying, "Oh, yeah, we have that too," and I say, "Oh yeah, of course, I guess we all have THE PASS, yeah," I give the nervous laugh, "Maybe next Friday."

At this time, I also start dating Niles and Maggie. They're the slightly off-center couple – a tall chick and a short British dude. He dyed her hair several different colors in the first few weeks of school. Their daughter is Charlotte, a Disney princess, with fair skin, dark hair, and beautiful dimples. I start talking to Niles because we're always there first to pick up our kids, alone, waiting for the doors to open. I have befriended the only two men that come to pick up their kids. No, the only two men my AGE. There are dads in their twenties, but I don't even speak the language. I just watch them on their Pretty Cloud, while I'm over on Tired and Old Cloud.

Niles and I talk about babysitters. We both don't have one, and then he's telling me we should swap each other's kids. I say I'd love to but Nathan never lets me leave him anywhere and then suddenly I'm invited to dinner with the kids. Niles tells me to bring them over, get Nathan used to Charlotte's house and then the next time I can leave him. When I leave preschool that day, my kids and I have dinner plans on Thursday, the zoo on Friday and now I'm dating the preschool parents.

As I head to my car, obviously giving off 'the vibe,' I'm approached by the perky mom with "angel" written in sparkles on her t-shirt. I wave, distantly. *I'm already seeing somebody,* I feel like saying, *in fact, three people, seven if you count spouses and kids.*

Our first date is Thursday, Charlotte's for dinner. I pack Nathan and two-year-old Emma in the car and go the ten blocks to their house on the hill. It's very clean – toys put away, pictures on the walls in an organized fashion; the couches aren't covered with dogs or stains. There's no chaos here.

Maggie greets me at the door, and then we're crowded into the doorway, the kids so happy they're silent, staring at each other. Niles is putting on kiddie music, the very kind I abhor the most, the <u>Children of the Corn</u> rendering of old favorites like "Itsy Bitsy Spider." Maggie doesn't give us any tour, in fact, she sort of blocks off the way to the rest of the house, so my kids and I divert our family river into the square of living room and pull out one box of trains, and suddenly there is every toy, the house is a mess and they bring me a cup of tea which I'd really like to have, and I set it to cool and of course never drink it, like with my own tea every morning. I find it at lunchtime, marooned next to the sink, *Oooohhhh tea, that would have been nice.* Then it's lunchtime and naptime and everyone's cranky and then after nap as the sun is going away, I start to feel like a failure – I'm not doing enough; I'm only doing laundry, cooking, breaking up fights, ushering dogs in and out, getting water for people.

We're in Charlotte and eighteen-month-old Audrey's room, which is really a strip of carpet between a bed and a crib and an avalanche of toys, stuffed into every crack and under beds and shelves, and the kids must play with every SINGLE one of the toys, especially toys that require a ladder to reach at the very tippy toppest of shelves, especially the imported toys from England which we find out later got lost. Then it's dinner time and Maggie relinquishes all control of the kitchen to me, to make my own plates from the steaming food, and I don't know her or her kitchen well enough to feel comfortable – it's like we haven't even gotten to first base and she's already walking around in a robe, disappointed, expecting me to get my own juice. That's intimate, man, going in someone's fridge. I don't know her maiden name, and I'm already handling her hot spaghetti, RIGHT ON THE STOVE in front of her.

Dinner consists of all of us cramming around a circular table. The kids eat about a thimble of spaghetti, the baby flips her juice with no lid so it splatters spectacularly in a star pattern on the floor. Niles cleans it up while Maggie tells him *I don't know why you gave her a cup with no lid*, then Audrey

HURLS the cup so it goes whizzing fractions of inches by my brain. My kids are delighted. They all run into the other room; Maggie chases after the loose baby, and Niles and I sit and eat the food off of everyone's plates until there's nothing left on the table. I can't talk. I feel insanely happy. It's washing over me, this relief that their life is as completely in the toilet socially as mine is.

Maggie comes back in, sits for a minute, shovels two forkfuls in, leaps up, zips out of the room as the baby scales the bookshelf. *Their life is a mess,* I think, happily. At my house, where I reenact this exact scene, every night, I'm irritated. At their house, the chaos is beautiful. Hilarious. A ballet. Niles and Maggie and I maybe get three minutes of really meaty conversation in. But our eyes are full with the knowledge. We are the same. We've swallowed our personal goals. We're sick with the indigestion of shattered hopes. We're swamped with kids, and their infinite freight trains of needs. Our eyes have a similar lost haze, an echo of who we once were until kids destroyed us. *We're perfect for each other.*

The next day at the zoo with Scott is my tougher date. I'm on my best behavior. This is THE friend, the one Nathan must have. I'm not as in sync with Scott, and the similarity to the old boyfriend, the one I ultimately left because, well, I HATED HIM, is starting to bug me. We follow the kids into the aviary, where they run through, fascinated with the million sets of double wire doors, to keep birds from escaping. It's like separate decompressions chambers, and impossible to get double strollers through. I eventually abandon my stroller altogether and lose myself in the maze, and after asking Scott every question about himself that I can think to ask to keep him busy talking, I wonder if maybe we're even going to see ONE bird. The aviary is apparently UNBURDENED with birds.

It turns out Scott is a marine biologist (while in actuality resembling a bouncer or pro wrestler) who, disillusioned with the corporate world of research, gave it all up to raise the kids while his wife works as a T.V. executive. We see lizards and sea lions. There are snacks. Michael and Nathan are dislocated into the whole experience, blissfully intimate. I'm trying hard and four hours later we're heading to the exit gates and I'm still not feeling it with Scott. I mean, it's all done with WORDS. We talk about the bedtimes, the diapers, the speed of childhood sprinting by…but I'm working hard to manufacture the feeling underneath, just like I did with my ex, Thomas, all those years ago, where I was pretty much dating my version of Thomas, when the real Thomas was just a guy who never talked. We were only eighteen. But wait a minute. *We're not REALLY dating.*

We reach the parking lot and I panic. Oh no! Did he have a good time? Are we going to see him again? Will Nathan get to go to his house? (The ultimate score.) Scott says, "We'll have to do this again," and I inwardly pop the cork. I scored the second date. Nathan will not die alone with no friends.

We plan another day to go the snow, and Scott looks thrilled. I realize I never see the man with his hands free, he's always holding the baby. Maybe I underestimate his ability to use gestures, maybe I should give him the tiniest break.

We say goodbye, head to our separate cars. I think about the boys running around together at the zoo. How they bared themselves easily, without thought. How excruciating it is to be vulnerable as an adult. I'm out of practice and awkward at being open – my own heart has rusted shut when it comes to new friends. Who could pick that lock?

I try not to fold the baby up in the stroller as Nathan uses my keys to simultaneously open and scratch up the hatchback. He sees Michael's car going by and reacts like an Italian seeing the Popemobile. He screeches "BEEP BEEP!" Scott beeps. Nathan blossoms. Baby Emma licks the window in gratitude.

Nathan looks excitedly at me, handing me the keys.

The Tortoise and the Hare

We have bunnies now. Not just one bunny. Two. They're fixed. I read that if you have two bunnies and they mate it takes thirty days and then you have ten babies; in four months those babies will mate, the female babies will have babies, and by the end of a year you can have a hundred and sixty rabbits.

NOW THAT'S WHAT I'M TALKIN' ABOUT. If only rabbits were bags of cash. But let's back up here.

The tortoise has died. We were leaving it alone, out in its outdoor pen, still feeding it, but the kindergarten teacher said her tortoise was hibernating, so we thought we should let Winky hibernate (okay, I thought we should, Nathan always thought it was a bad idea. He wanted Winky to sleep with us, go the grocery store, take bike rides). Anyway, the Wink was living outside, eating the lettuce I'd fling out for him, but tortoises are so slow and spend so much time in their shell that I could never tell if he was happy or just slow-ly dying, and it turns out – whoops – inching towards death.

We hadn't had him out in awhile and I thought, screw this hibernation, he keeps moving around in his little out-door hutch so he can't be hibernating. Every time I throw food in, he's in a different spot. So I said, "Let's take Winky to the park with us," and the kids are thrilled, and we pick him up and put him in the day-glo pink crate that's made for Pound Puppies, those stuffed toys. We get on the bike; there's the yelling about who gets to sit in the front; there's the crying; there are the threats; there's the usual "That's it, we're not GOING to the park," then we're off.

We're meeting Charlotte and Audrey and Niles, and the day is blooming. It's seventy degrees in December, the kids are playing on the monkey bars, sharing Cheetos. Charlotte has four new fairy dolls to share; Emma has a rolling pin and some tin pans, which she refuses to share, Audrey wants to be swung on the swings, and Niles and I talk about how to make money.

I try to convince Nathan to eat some ham sandwiches, but no one wants to eat. He hasn't eaten since, like, Thanksgiving when he got the stomach flu.

Then I go over to get Winky out and I just have this feeling. Haven't really looked at him in awhile. I take him out. He looks the same. His arms and legs move when I move them. But I look in at his head. I stare in there. It looks like his eyelids are missing. Like a skull, he doesn't have any eyes. I start having a really bad feeling. Maybe tortoises just look like that.

Nathan comes over. I say, "Uhh, I'm not sure Winky's doing okay."

"What Mom?" He can't hear anything; he's had an ear infection, and can't hear out of his right ear.

I look at Nathan. "Something's wrong with his eyes."

Nathan looks at Winky. But he's looking at the look on my face, and that worries him.

I say, "His eyelids are missing. I'm not sure he's still alive."

"What Mom?"

This sucks. He loves this tortoise. Did I kill it? It never felt like lettuce was enough to feed it. We gave it broccoli too. We gave it apples, beans, all things it said to give it, we gave it. We left it alone because the teacher said to leave it alone. *He died from heartbreak.*

Emma comes over. I have to break it to her. I say gently, "I'm not sure he's alive anymore. He doesn't look right." Nathan's heart is shattering into a million pieces, falling around his bare feet like hard candy. I say we have to take him home to Daddy, maybe Daddy will know. I try to pack up the bike. We don't say anything to Niles about the tortoise, about how we brought a dead tortoise to the park to play – and he's oblivious, calling, "Say bye to Winky! Bye Winky! Take good care of that tortoise!" Every word is like a gunshot in our hearts. Nathan's looking at Niles with horror. I can't pack the bike fast enough.

On the way home, Nathan's saying "Maybe he's okay. Why does he have to die?" I told him maybe he was sick. The teacher said he did look kind of thin when we brought him in to show and tell. The teacher had tortoises, she knew them better than we did.

"He wasn't sick," Nathan says.

I say, "We found him on the road. Maybe he was looking for a place to go because he wasn't doing too well, Nathan...and then he got to be in our family for the last few months of his life. He got to have a good place to be." I try to sound hopeful.

We get home and Gramma and Daddy can't tell if the tortoise is dead either. It doesn't look good. But the tortoise is missing his EYES. He's not moving. I say we have to bury him. Nathan is distraught, but also looks for the shovel.

We find a spot out by the fig tree and hope the dogs won't dig him up. We start digging. Nathan doesn't want to leave him in the ground. I tell him that when the body dies, there's a spirit inside the animal or the person that goes out, that the spirit gives you all your life and happiness. When that leaves, all that's left is the shell, the body, and the body is made of water and dust and if you put it back in the dirt, it'll make other tortoises. He looks at me and says "How?" I say "Well, not make other tortoises, but grow grass that will feed other tortoises." Then I start to tell him about how we're all made of earth and stars and he says, "Can I have a band aid?" Then we bury the tortoise, and say nice things about him – that we love him – and Nathan is sitting next to the hole, looking terrible, in his black wedding pants and his dress black jacket we got at Half-Price Wednesday at the local thrift store, and he says, "I'm sad," and then he cries. I sit next to him in the dirt and put my arm around him, and he says, "Why does he have to die?" and I don't know either. I cry too. I just tell him it's okay to be sad, that means you loved him. I curse myself for having no real religion.

Then we're going to the animal shelter to look at bunnies for a possible tortoise replacement, even though I know this is wrong, to fill the hole, instead of letting healing fill the hole. But I'm doing it anyway because Nathan was crying. Nathan says from the dark backseat, "I didn't even make Winky a Christmas stocking," in a cracking voice, and at five, already feels regret.

We look at bunnies but don't get one, and the next day online I see a posting for free bunnies that will be euthanized if they're not rescued by Friday. So I contact the woman, and we head to the animal shelter after nap. The kids are excited. (Although, they are still mournful about Winky.)

We get to the bunny area, and Emma is interested in the bunnies for about three minutes before she takes her skirt up around her neck and dances around singing, "I'm wearing my skirt on my neck," and takes her shoes off in the dirty parking lot, wearing thin black tights and a pink leotard, her sweater already discarded on top of the doll and the plastic bucket we brought to take the bunny home in. Nathan is more focused; he looks in all the cages. The Bunny Rescue Lady is dressed like a Christmas realtor, and is showing us all the bunnies. Nathan likes a white one that climbs on him named Twix, and Emma starts screaming, I WANT A GIRRRRRL BUNNY! And the lady tells us boy bunnies fight, so there's really only one already fixed girl bunny who seems nice, a loaf of yellow fur bread. There are two really big girl bunnies, laying together and looking like a pair of size eleven bunny slippers, but Nathan has picked his, and the lady says it's better if there are two bunnies, to keep each other company. So now we're getting two bunnies. We're pretty sure we've decided, but we follow her to the back for the last room of bunny choices. We go through a hallway that has a giant snake in it, a ferret (a carrot? Emma says), and two bunnies who just gave birth, where we see the smallest rabbits I've ever seen – two day old bunnies, like real bunnies, but matchstick size. Pocket bunnies.

Then we're in the secret backyard of the shelter and there are three raggedy goats – goats in North Hollywood! – and more bunnies, the kind that look like Peter Rabbit, but the kids have already made their decision. Emma is starting to scream and cry about everything because it's almost dinner time and it's her new thing to cry and say her legs hurt and she can't walk, you have to pick her up.

We get back to the bunnies, show her the ones we like, and the lady pops off to get the paperwork. Nathan and I look in the cages while Emma flounces off onto the loading ramp, and some guy in a brown animal cops uniform with an impressive heavy belt comes around the corner and tells me I have to reign in my free-range Emma – she's pushing the safety boundary. Even though there's nowhere for her to go, no traffic or danger, he points out that the really Bad Dogs are locked up back there – way back there, by the sheep, behind a huge, locked, chain link gate with barbed wire on top. I try to impress upon her the safety issue, but she sees the guy is an overreacting fake, looks at the walkie talkie on his belt, and then resumes skipping around. At least a little closer.

Bunny Realtor comes back with boxes for the bunnies, puts some hay in the boxes, we get the bunnies in, we get to the car, there's hugging. I'm starting to regret the whole bunny experience, realizing I'm now going to be taking care of two bunnies. The kids are screaming as soon as we get back on the road, tired and still sick with runny noses they got as soon as school broke for vacation.

I say we can rename the bunnies, and suggest Christmas. Nathan loves that; he names his Christmas. Then Emma says, "I'll call mine Thanksgiving!" Then she decides, "No, Christmas Eve!" But then she settles on Cinderella. Christmas thumps the ground when he's happy. Out in the barn, out of a cage for the first time in months, he leaps in the air, twists around, thumps the ground.

When Daddy gets home we have Cinderella and

Christmas in the bed watching <u>The Grinch</u> with the kids. Barry is horrified. Farm animals in bed.

In bed later that night, in the dark, the bunnies safe in their habitat in the barn, Nathan, who can barely hear, says, "Do you think the tortoise was looking forward to die?"

The dark swallows us, and his question.

Daddy says to him, "You loved him, and you were good to him, and that's all you can do, Nathan."

Ski School
or
Here, Carry More Stuff

Nathan is four and a half, and Emma just turned three yesterday, and we're visiting Daddy who's working on a sports show that's filming on a snow-buried mountain.

"You should take them to ski school," he encourages.

"Come on, let's go out to the snow!"

"YEAH! OKAY MOM!"

They scramble around and take off their pajamas, and then play in the closet and throw the toys down into the living room from the new-found loft launch pad upstairs. An hour later they're still "makid."

"Don't you want to go to the snow?"

"YEAH!" Great idea! Again! No movement to get dressed. Four years in, every single day we get dressed, and yet there's no learned behavior there. It's like a Christmas surprise everyday.

I shove clothing over heads. More clothing. Then the ski clothing. Brush the hair. Screaming. Bribery. Hats on. Coats. Scarves. Gloves.

I feel like I've been through a hurricane aimed directly in my face, and we haven't left the house yet. Still they look so cute in their snow clothes, I have to take a picture. I push my irritation at them to a small corner of my brain where I'm storing it all for later. (I have a warehouse.)

We drive the hundred feet from our condo to the sign marked Ski School because I found out yesterday that Emma takes three steps in snow before yelling "My legs hurt! Carry me!"

As we get out of the car, I stuff the two cameras, video and still, money, keys, I.D. and A.T.M. card, lip stuff, water jug, Kleenex, three pairs of sunglasses, and gum all in my coat pockets. There's no place for the three huge carrots I brought as a snack. I know it's a mistake leaving them.

There is no clearly marked entrance, so we climb up a two-minivan-high mountain of snow (carrying Emma and dragging Nathan) to find that we're in the back of the building, and have to slide down an enormous ice wall to certain death to get to the entrance. It's better than going back. We slide down, landing on other people going in.

Inside, everyone is twenty-one and from New Zealand. I pay about six hundred dollars for the equipment rental and the use of an Austrian guy named Augustine to teach us to ski. Inside the building the kids are burning hot, so now my pockets are stuffed with all our gloves, three hats, and two scarves.

We go to get fitted for skis. Actually, only the kids, my skis are in another building, which I can SEE from this building, but which I can not get to, with two kids whose legs are broken in snow. Cassie, the sassy Australian, volunteers to help get their boots, so I can run over and get my own skis, at another enormous cost to me. Nathan starts crying, certain I am leaving him in the ski school forever.

I get my own skis, boots, and poles. There's something wrong. The feeling starts when the guy HANDS me poles and skis, lift tickets, and receipts. Here, *carry more stuff.*

I walk back across to the kiddie building. I can barely walk in these concrete boots made from hell. I've only skied once before, on a school trip at seventeen. Now I remember why.

I get there and the kids are ready. It's now a little past eleven. We should in actuality be DONE now, taking off our clothes and putting on our other clothes for the walk to the lunch place, which is twenty steps away and will take us an hour. But I decide it's vacation, Barry said "Ski school is good; they'll love it," so I'm going to believe him.

Augustine meets us in the outdoor kiddie area. "HELLO, NATTAN, and EMMA." He can barely speak English. He's fresh from Heidi and Grandfather's mountain. He sits down with them in the snow, setting their feet straight, toes pointed up.

"Can you see this looks like French fries?" Then he tilts his own feet 'til they point in, toes together. "And this looks like pizza? Can you make pizza?"

Emma is eating snow and Nathan is looking at the passing snow plow.

"Can you make pizza?"

Now Emma is looking around for pizza.

I feel like shaking them. I PAID FOUR HUNDRED DOLLARS. MAKE PIZZA.

They turn their toes in.

"GOOD!"

First they ski with one ski down the little hill. One at a time, Augustine shepherds them to the top, skis down with one, goes back up, gets the orphaned one at the top, brings her down. I see what I must look like. Running from one to the other. Helping. All day. *I look like an idiot.*

They make it down on two skis. I decide it's time to put on my own skis. I shove all the cameras in my pockets. Can I ski with this much stuff in my pockets? If I fall to the left, I have to buy a new videocamera. I decide to do all my falling to the right.

I get my feet in the skis. I flashback to the horror of being seventeen. I'm strapped to sticks, on ice, and I'm unpopular. I watch three-year-old Emma going down the hill by herself, with Augustine close behind.

I dig my poles in and try to heave myself out of the cordoned-off kiddie area. I'm sweating and I haven't moved at all. I take off my skis and throw them over the rope. Nathan thinks I'm trying to escape. "Where you going, Mommy?"

I get to the other side, and put the skis back on. At least

it's flat. I try to look casual.

Emma has gone down the hill three times. She's crying now. She needs food. THOSE CARROTS. I curse myself. But we paid for Augustine. We're going on the ski lift.

"Do you think we can go up the big hill?"

He looks at the lift. "Sure!"

It takes us a lifetime to get to the lift. Emma is crying, hates skiing, is done with the whole snow scene. There are no princess movies here, no chance to be naked.

Nathan keeps trying to walk, and keeps crossing his skis over and falling into broken leg pretzel shapes. I try to lift them up while they cry and beg me to help them, but I can hardly move myself.

At the chair lift, the kids want to go with me. Augustine says we would surely die, and gets on with the two kids, while I get on the chair behind him. For the ride to the top, it's silent, white, and beautiful.

As we near the top, he tries to get the attention of the kid in the booth to slow down the lift, but the guy is reading and doesn't hear anything, so Augustine jumps mightily off the lift with the two kids, and they tumble off into a giant snow drift. Emma cries now. Oh wait, she never stopped crying.

I can't ski, I suddenly realize, and I have to get off the chair. And this is the bunny slope? I don't know what kind of bunnies they have around here, this slope is immense.

I get off the chair and try to make pizza. My hips feel like they're coming out of their sockets. I tumble onto the pile of children and Austrian.

As we untangle ourselves, Emma holds her arms out so I'll carry her. I look at her like she's crazy. Augustine looks at me excitedly. "Can you ski without poles?"

"Oh. Um...." *NO.*

"Or can you ski holding her?" He's holding out Emma.

"I'VE ONLY SKIED ONCE," I tell him.

He looks undaunted. Looks down the mountain. Thinking positively.

Emma holds her arms out to me. "Honey, I can't carry you. I don't know how to ski. That's why we have Augustine."

She can't fathom that there's something I can't do.

"Okay, Nattan, hold my hand. You are going to make pizza down the mountain. Okay? You ready?" He hefts up Emma.

They start down the hill. I start sliding down behind them. *Please, I can't die.* They glide way ahead of me, a smooth Austrian ski team. My legs are warped by my supremely unnatural, hip wrenching pizza-making stance. I stay on my feet the whole way, in great pain, because MOMMY CAN'T DIE.

At the bottom Augustine looks exhilarated even though Emma is still crying and Nathan has fallen like an octopus around his legs. This must be his version of success. I admire his foreign world.

He shakes my hand enthusiastically. Says goodbye to the kids.

We watch our pillar of strength stride off. The kids and I try to ski the twenty steps to the lunch place. We can't get anywhere. I take off all our skis, and then I'm carrying Emma, three sets of skis, and two poles. I curse Barry. Sure, take them to ski school! I'm loaded with nineteen extra awkward things, AND it's snowing, everyone's hungry, and their hip sockets are swollen.

We eat lunch, we drink the healing hot chocolate, we head back the twenty steps to drop off all our skis. At step fifteen, Emma just falls on the snow and won't get up. I leave her and Nathan, go inside, dump our stuff, get our boots, run back over past my pile of lifeless kids, drop off my own stuff, get my own boots, get back to the kids. I feel my burn out meter being reached, or wait, I reached it sometime after breakfast, three years ago. I vomit the load of boots, hats, gloves, scarves from my arms all around them. I can caddy no more.

I look at them strewn on the ground.

Emma is face down, happily licking the fresh snow. Nathan lays on his back, picking the bark off a tree, the falling snowflakes melting on his cheeks. They look refreshed, red-cheeked, like Santa's elves.

"Did you taste it?" Emma looks at me, eyes shiny,

showing me her tongue.

My muscles are shredded to toothpicks. *Why have I done this whole trip?!*

"Taste it," she tells me.

I collapse next to Nathan. The skiers ending their runs zoom past us. A hardy Norwegian group passes, singing. Plows go by. I look up and all I see is white, a deluge falling through the trees – heavy unstoppable sheets of it – snow swirling in thick, slow motion. But by the time it reaches us we barely feel it, the snow's immensity reduced to dots of tiny mouse footprints. I surrender. I stick out my tongue like Emma. I feel a cold cheek next to mine.

"I think it's what clouds taste like," Nathan says.

He Rides Off

People are so busy they're hiring other people to teach their kids fundamental things, like learning to ride a bike. 'Bike coaches' they're called. People are too busy for this?

I admit, I don't want to do it myself. It seems too hard, and there's running involved. The training wheels are getting loud and loose on Nathan's bike; he's almost done with pre-school; he's four and a half; I know it's time. But how can anyone teach the balancing, the pedaling? It's intricate. I don't know how *I* do it. Still, we take the training wheels off. It requires pliers, which thrills Nathan. I try running with him in our back driveway, holding the back of the bike about ten times as he pedals. It's hard to run all bent over, holding someone up, especially someone you'd rather not see all scraped up when he crashes into the wall. He pedals a few times before almost falling and I realize I should probably teach him braking before anything else. Good to go, but can't go forever. Better to know how to stop once going.

Nathan is then in the netherworld where his training wheels are off, but he doesn't know how to ride the bike. The bike leans against the plastic pirate ship in the backyard for weeks. Nathan is graduating from preschool. It is hot. We don't have time for another lesson. Neither of us really LIKE the lessons. He starts riding the tricycle again, the now only-functioning-bike. I have succeeded in regressing him.

We try again. Out front, with a helmet on. I run along-side, holding the seat, telling him to look where he's going. Telling him to practice braking. Slowly letting go for seconds at a time. He's improving. He can go a little while before I catch him or he crashes into the curb. He gets half a block one time. It's happening. I call Barry out with the video camera. This is before I spilled milk into the video camera, and it still worked.

As Barry holds the camera, I help Nathan get going (he still needs help balancing and gaining speed), and then he rides off slowly. Then he slows enough to put his feet down to drag himself to a stop. He needs help at the beginning and the end, but he can do the middle, the balancing, by himself.

The next night we're out practicing. This time I want to see him go. I keep saying, "Let me help you get started, so you can go really fast," but he isn't interested; he has other ideas. He wants to keep practicing the boring part, the start-ing part, standing with the bike under him, getting the pre-cision of lifting his feet, one at a time, balancing enough to start his bike, pedaling, before it falls over. He isn't getting anywhere. I stand helplessly in the middle of the street.

I'm so frustrated. I want him to see how fast he can go; the fun of going fast will give him more desire to learn to ride. Barry stands over near Emma, who is riding around on her Princess bike, still with training wheels, way too big for her. She is on a ten minute monologue to convince us that she can have her training wheels off, too.

I retreat back to Barry and sit down on the curb. As we are eaten alive by ants, I complain that Nathan won't do it my way. This isn't the way I pictured it. WHERE IS THE PROGRESS? Emma makes large lazy circles in front of us with her purple bike, making the double rolling sound of hard training wheels on a silent street. I look over at Nathan. I look at him on his bike. The sun is going down. He is stopped. He's walking awkwardly with the bike between his legs, rolling until one pedal sticks up. He balances on one foot, putting the other foot on the high pedal. He's wobbling, but trying to get his bottom foot on. He gets them both on and then the bike starts to fall, so he puts both feet down. Then he starts over. And over. And over. Again. My frenzy starts to melt away. My brain somehow begins to shrink down to this one moment. I suddenly realize that this is the only day he's going to be struggling with the bike. The time spent learning something is a millisecond compared to the time spent doing it once you learn it. *How could this be?* Nathan is right. He doesn't need to ride fast today. He's going to be riding fast the rest of his life. He's never going to be at this wobbly stage again. This is it.

I don't do anything. I watch him. I watch Emma, and I watch Barry, slapping ants, out with us in the sun. Hardly any cars come by. The street is ours. The world is ours.

He practices awhile, and then we go in to get ready for bed. He doesn't ride fast that day, in fact he never even gets anywhere. He just practices, on his own, learning to start off.

The next day, like I knew, he rides off.

Elementary School

The Practice of Leaving

The backpacks are ready. They're sitting on the bike chain in case we ride to the new big school on our bikes tomorrow. Nathan hasn't decided. Daddy would have to ride Bruce's bike. We packed the Wiggles backpack with his Spiderman notebook, in which are placed four extra-sharpened Spidey pencils, two handkerchiefs (for crying – I may need both), three pictures of the family so he won't forget us (one was of the four of us by the pool, and Nathan decided we had to cut out the bottom of the picture so everyone at school wouldn't see him naked – he likes to skinnydip), and three pieces of paper. He also packed his stuffed Eeyore who has spent the summer on the floor of the living room like a rug no one cared about, and a tractor pulling a trailer. He's also taking a piece of paper with his phone number on it, and one dollar and thirty cents for lunch and milk.

Emma packed nothing, I packed her a change of clothes and her Little Mermaid and Prince Eric dolls. She probably won't even crack the suitcase. And Nathan has no idea who Spiderman or the Wiggles are, he never watches the cartoons. One of the Wiggles was at a birthday party we went to once, so that's why he picked the backpack.

There are uniforms at his school, even though it's a public one. Blue shorts and white or blue shirts. He wore the uniform a few days last week, he was so excited about it. I just hope that tomorrow I can either stop crying, or start crying, but after he's already in class. The whole experience is so large, motherhood, it's like being an astronomer. Everything happens in the dark; you're feeling around and then there are these beautiful comets.

I can't remember much of kindergarten. I don't remember my teacher's name. Mrs. Brucker? I remember her wearing a really horrific gold high-collared shirt. And I remember being IN LOVE with Miss Griffiths, my second grade teacher. She had red hair and was tall and beautiful. I used to write her love notes. I think back on it, and imagine how she was probably about thirty years old, and here was a seven-year-old in love with her, the whole idea of her.

I remember that little hallway from the kindergarten to the rest of the school – outside, by the pretend wooden stove area. And I remember the bathroom because I ate lunch in there one year when I was, no doubt, older and wiser.

I remember nap time where we got to sleep on little mats on the floor and the teacher would wake us up with a little fairy wand. I loved that paste too. And this boy Kris Matzel would always want to hold my hand at recess and I thought he was an idiot. He had a bad haircut and squinty eyes. The first graders used to come up to the fence and yell "kindergarten babies, born in the navy" through the fence at us.

Life is so much this strange experiment where you're looking at things through a cocoon of growing up. I swear I still didn't know what I was doing, even in college. I was still standing in the sandbox wondering why all the loser guys always wanted to hold my hand. I'm so much more evolved now.

We've spent the summer swimming, riding bikes and scooters – me on the treadmill or reading while the kids zoomed around on their bikes. There have been plenty of fights to break up, naps to wrestle the kids down for.

Lying in bed tonight after Emma was crying because she couldn't have any pudding – she was suddenly starving and then went to sleep – I just watched Nathan and scratched his head as he tossed and turned, and then we talked about what his friend Michael might bring to school tomorrow – maybe his Stitch toy that he brought in preschool – and here is his little earnest face, big eyes, white blanket hair. He's five years old, the tiny meatloaf baby, whose face gets flat and round when he cries, he's trying to be so big, and I know I'll feel this way in college. He's just this little boy. We cling to him, all of us crammed in the bed, because that auditorium is going to be big tomorrow, and he's going to line up like all the other kids, but this is my life, these sections of coming and going, the practice of leaving, where he comes back… I'm cherishing the coming back right now.

Home Cooking

I saw that there was a cooking class offered at the rec center, and mentioned it to fellow mom Maggie, who said she wanted to take it too, with her two girls. But the time was right at naptime, and Nathan was in kindergarten and would miss out altogether. I knew he liked cooking from the Mommy and Me class we did where no one else showed up and it truly was just mommy and me and the teacher, and all we did each week was cook.

We picked Thursday for our own private cooking day at home. We were up at seven, eating breakfast, getting dressed, biking to school, then taking Emma back to the house so I could run on the treadmill while she watched Eloise, then back on the bike to drop her at preschool, then back to the car to run to the store to buy all the things for the recipes I looked up online. Taking way too long shopping, rushing home, shoving everything cold in the fridge in the plastic bags, leaving the rest on the counters still packed up, jumping on the bike to pump up to school to get my visitor's pass, to park my bike illegally by the kindergarten door, to get into class to sit on the rug while the teacher reads a story. Then we're painting pumpkins, I'm outside, with strangers' children, holding buckets of orange paint while they paint on the easel which we have to keep moving to keep it in the shade, and then I'm saying, *First write your name. Then draw a big circle, really big. Huge. Then paint in orange.* The kids tell me what they're going to be for Halloween. Spiderman is big with the boys. Fairies and unicorns and princesses for the girls.

I don't get to finish all the kids painting because we run out of time and it's time to get in line for lunch, and Nathan's eyes are looking for me; he's waving in his half-shy way to say "Come on, Mom!" and I say I have to clean up, I'll be right there, and I clean and then go to where they're all lined up at picnic tables eating their lunches, and how am I this old, that I can be at a lunch at an elementary school where I'm not the kid? And there's MY kid, and he's the best one. How lucky is that?

I open milks, that's the biggest job of lunch helper. And I try and get kids to eat a little more. I like all the kids; they're all sweet. I look at them and picture them old, as accountants, and dry cleaners store owners and moms and bicycle repairmen and postal workers.

Then there's trash to put away, and the lining back up to go outside and play, and there's my boy, holding my hand because he's only five, and he's proud to hold my hand, the only kid in that great long line that has his mom there. And I have to leave to pick up Emma and he hugs and kisses me, and then tells me to hug Norman, and then "hug all the kids"

and they all hug me and laugh and head in to the playground, their favorite part of the day (although Nathan is
pretty serious and works very hard on his writing and
authoring books). I'm learning that even though I feel like I
live in my head all the time, organizing things – time, food,
children – that with kindergarten, Nathan and I have adjust-
ed to things together, him getting used to longer hours,
being in a group of kids, trusting that I'll still be there, and
me, getting used to him in the group of kids, that the group
is made up of all these excellent children, but that I'm feeling things first, and leaving the figuring out for later. Because
the feeling is enormous, with all those fresh five-year-old
buns from the oven. They take you on their ride. You are
their guide, and their ride. It's remarkable, and a little like a
hippie commune.

Then I run and get Emma and have some guilt because
she's at preschool instead of with me, and then we rush
home and I put the groceries away while she watches <u>Eloise</u>,
and I cook chicken, and cut up veggies, and prepare salmon,
and then I'm late getting her to nap, and she resists nap, and
I hate that, then it's too late for a nap but we lie down anyway. She's almost asleep but I have to go pick up Nathan so
she misses her nap, and then we're getting Nathan on the
bike, and it's hot, and we finish all the food prep and we go
swimming while Nathan plays music, and then Maggie and
her family come over, and the cooking class is happening

and I've never been busier, but I was made for this – this life was made for me. Even as a little kid, I knew, I wanted to be a mom.

Then wait, I'm doing all the cooking, and even when the kids come over I'm still doing all the cooking, and I see why you'd pay forty bucks a kid for a cooking class for eight weeks. Because I'm doing all the cooking just like I normally do all the cooking, but now I'm doing it and trying to make it fun, which is twice as much work, and an eighth as much fun, but it's a slim eighth; it might be worth it if I didn't try so hard to make it so happy and instead just let it be. I manage to cook a dinner and a dessert, and the kids like to help and make their own foods, but the cooking class lasts about nine minutes, total, and the rest is me picking cheese out of my hair while doing a shitload more dishes, my feet aching, the food baking. The kids really just want to take off all their clothes and play in the pirate ship outside, or chase each other on bikes, or get into fights, or cry or swing or try on princess outfits. They want to celebrate being together, on a weeknight, an ordinary Thursday in October. The cooking is a decoration for their event – to huddle in front of a new tiny T.V. that Daddy brought home from work. To huddle. This is the event. Not the cheese and broccoli or the apples we smash up or the cinnamon.

They eat the salmon I made and the adults eat the pastry with the meat inside that the kids made. Milk is spilled instantly. The kids take a bite of the apples and declare them disgusting. They eat store-bought ice cream instead and decide that that's the best part of cooking class. We clean up and talk a little. We're making it good for them, since they have rare cousins that visit, this is an alternative to play and feel part of a community. I like Maggie and her family. It's nice to be in bed tired at the end of the day with a smile on my face from a new adventure. It's warmer in the house with the oven going.

Learning to Swim from a Three-Year-old

Take off all your clothes.

Laugh.

Have someone nearby who knows what they're doing.

Only go in as far as it's safe.

Stay there a long time, like a month.

Really enjoy it there.

Then tell the person to back up.

Have them know you well enough to say "Come here!"

See that they're not far.

Try swimming towards them.

Be caught. Be celebrated.

Be placed back on the steps.

Let the person show you to hold your fingers together, stuck like glue, like a fin, so you travel faster.

Stand up.

Look at the person.

Laugh excitedly.

Make your hands into fins.

(Show the person your hands if you want, to celebrate this knowledge.)

Jump.

Keep your head up.

Look where you're going.

It's not that far. It's only a few inches.

Do this for a month.

Slowly the person moves farther back, only a step.

You're really only barely above the water.

But you like the feeling.

You're safe, and independent at once.

Go to the deep end and try the same thing with your person.

Watch your big brother swim with goggles.

Get some goggles.

Put your head under the water.

Play on the steps with the goggles, floating, looking underwater, able to stand when you need to.

Swim holding your nose with your head under and goggles on, to your person.

About a thousand times.

This is really the key, the practice.

Then, suddenly, stick your head under and swim across the deep end, with and without goggles, without help, with your person nearby, a perfect, comfortable lap all on your own, like magic, like you've been swimming easily all your life.

Get to the step, stand up and say "Can I do that again?"

The Family Bed
or
You'll Never Go to the Movies at Night Again

We never meant to have a family bed. There was a time I didn't even know what that was. Before I was a parent, when I was a nanny, I would have thought the idea ridiculous, too hippie, too messy. I liked that the parents went out at night, that the kids were regimented to their rooms, that they stayed in bed, everything nice and tidy, leaving me a quiet night on the sofa reading in a thick sweater.

Nathan slept in his own crib until he was seven months. Then I started getting lazy. I nursed him in bed. I had discovered nursing while lying on your side in bed, which was my downfall, or upfall. I'd fall asleep, he'd fall asleep, Barry would crawl in on the other side, boom, Family Bed. Nathan started liking to fall asleep on my arm, holding on to my elbow. He's five years old now, and still obsessed with the elbow. Gives it a good pinch right before sleeping. Daddy's elbows are better than mine. More stretchy. We started watching movies with Nathan sprawled asleep between us. Then the next baby came, and there was a look on Nathan's eighteen-month-old face, when I squeezed two-day old Emma in the bed and shoved him over a tiny bit. *You replaced me.*

Emma likes to fall asleep clutching a handful of my "cold" hair. She feels around until she finds the coldest pieces, and then holds on and falls asleep.

We spent hours together cooking today, which was good except for all the cooking. And at one point I was playing "Duck, Duck Goose" in my son's kindergarten playground, outside the room in which he's grown into a sturdy five years old in, in one month. I get in bed, tired. The kids and Barry are already there, everyone pjayed and teethbrushed and talking, chattering, about this thing at school, or this person, and the talking descends into jibber jabber, and then they start kicking each other, "She touched me!" "No I didn't. He's LYING." "Don't say LYING," we threaten. Barry gets out of the bed, Nathan calls and cries for him to come back. We tell them to be quiet. I sing a song while Nathan says "pencil pencil pencil flower flower flower" to try and mess me up. Then more threats, then Nathan flips his body around more; Emma cries; the last trips to the bathroom; Nathan saying to Emma to "Get back onboard!" Emma using my foot to grapple back up on the bed to her hole in the blankets. More crazy conversation and then there's a calm that surfaces and spreads across the bed. It's accidental. It's inevitable as the clock's hands surging forward. The silence of not quite sleep. Emma's eyes blinking heavily, Nathan nestled in next to Barry, squeezing his elbow,

"I love you Daddy," then the total silence of sleep.

Barry gets out of the bed like a cat, rolling and snaking away to go and eat something, and I lay there exhausted, and watch my thoughts mist out of my brain and up into the ceiling fan to dissipate, and I slowly melt back into myself, the best parts of the day sifting down. Emma's legs are thrown over mine, her fist in my hair. Nathan is lying on my shoulder. It's like lying in the middle of hot cinnamon rolls – cozy, swirled, iced, a beehive complexity, just us. I feel their warmth and peace floating on our family raft, and this is my payment for the tough day, a get well card, my wish for tomorrow, slung and strewn across me and breathing asleep.

We hardly see Nathan now, he's at school so much. I think we all look forward to our leap into bed at night. The book or the T.V. surfing (Animal Planet), the lights out, the nightlight on. The fight about whose turn it is to turn the nightlight on, the fight about whose turn it is to sleep in the middle, the crying of the person whose turn it is to sleep next to the wall, or next to the edge, the dreaded edge, the only place where there's actually enough room to sleep.

They'll be sick of us in no time. They'll move to their own beds. My doctor said her daughter slept in bed with them until she was six. The kid's bedroom was merely for show, or guests. Nathan's already figured out that he'd be fine to sleep on his own, he'd just miss Dad's elbow. I've thought about getting a mannequin arm and rigging up some sort of fleshy elbow, but I think at some point (maybe at the point mannequins become involved) you gotta draw the line.

For now we're enjoying the crowd. So we miss a few movies. Matinees are cheaper anyway.

Dead Bunnies Are Easier to Carry

Emma's bunny is dying. She hopped sideways for three weeks, and then she stopped getting up except to lurch around in the cage, and now the very last of her lying there, next to her buddy Christmas, her white best friend for the last six months, who has stuck with her to the end. I check on her lots of times the last day, and feel guilty even though the vet says no heroic measures. It's a rabbit, living its natural end. She's had six great months of not living at the pound, where we got her, living with her friend Christmas, and living cage free during the day, hopping around and eating vegetables. I try to look at it that way.

When I go in at dusk, she is laying there not breathing. Nathan looks at my face to see if it is bad. "Is Emma's bunny okay?" he asks.

"No…," I say, feeling terrible.

I open the cage, and feel her. She is soft, but not alive.

"We have to bury her," I say.

Emma is sad that her bunny died. She stands on the treadmill when I tell her. "She scratched," she says. Her bunny has always been the wilder one. Hard to hold, hard to catch and, as I will find out soon, she was the one that ate most of the food and made most of the mess in the cage.

Destructo Rabbit, she would fling around the food dish and shred the newspapers. Christmas, it turns out, is the ideal bunny. Doesn't bite. Lives a clean bachelor's life. And with Cinderella safe in heaven, he will come in the house more and hang out with us, because it's easier to watch one bunny and make sure he doesn't chew the phone wires, than it is to watch two.

We dig a hole out by the fig tree, where we buried the tortoise, Winky, and the fish, Book. It is becoming the Death section of the yard. The bunny is big, so the hole has to be big, and the ground isn't soft and yielding as it always looks in pioneer movies when they have to bury someone. Those cowboys are so burly, or they're better shovelers. Either way, I strain, and the hole is dug.

Emma goes into the garage with me to get the bunny. I feel stricken, seeing Cinderella lying there, still dead. I'm the only one feeling bad because I'm the only one who spent time with the bunnies, feeding and taking care of them each morning and night. I get attached, while Nathan, one day, tells me, "I don't really like the bunnies so much. I get something and after about a month, I don't care about it so much anymore."

I take the bunny's body out of the cage, wrapping it in a clean white diaper rag from the kitchen. Emma says "I wanna carry her, Mommy." I feel weird about it, the bunny is dead. Could children carry dead things? But she wants to do it, and it isn't diseased, so I hand her the bunny, feeling torn. As I follow her out the garage door, I almost laugh, realizing that this is the first time Emma is carrying her bunny easily. This bunny scratched and wiggled, she was very hard for a kid to hold on to. I have found the best pet for any four-year-old. Dead rabbit!

When we get to the hole, Emma immediately *heaves* the body into the grave. Her first burial, Emma is radically unaware of graveside etiquette. After recovering from my shock at her technique, I kneel down and explain gently to her that when you love something, you try and bury it carefully, you maybe don't HEAVE it into the hole. We have to dig the hole a little bigger and deeper because this bunny is big and I don't want the dogs digging it up an hour after we bury her.

Emma helps me put her in gently, still wrapped in the rag. Then we sprinkle some grass on top of her, 'cause we figure she liked grass. And I tell Emma she could say something nice about the bunny. She says, "She was a great bunny." Then we fill the dirt in on top.

Nathan comes out from the bathroom where he's been holed up, and is distressed that he's missed the burial. Even more distressed that I've buried the rag along with the bunny, because we use those rags.

The next day I miss the bunny, then the next day the

hole she's left is filled in slightly, then the next day I start focusing on the one good bunny we have left, being glad for that bunny. One day they're here, the next day, maybe not. And with death, it seems you'll never get used to the space that's left, and then, sadly, you do. The space fills in.

Three days later, Nathan says to me, "Can we dig up Emma's bunny and play with it?"

Paul Small

In bed, we're laying four across like thick railroad ties. Nathan and Emma in the middle, me and Barry risking the outer edges.

It's pretty quiet. It's a Thursday, the book has been read, the light turned off; Nathan's wearing a T-shirt and boxers in the middle of winter, Emma's in her princess pjs that she hasn't taken off in two days.

Nathan says, "Why'd you pick my name?"

"We liked that name."

He's quiet.

"Don't you like that name?"

"No. I want a different name."

"Like what?"

He thinks. "…Paul."

"Paul?!"

He nods.

"Why?" I'm wondering who at school is named Paul, where he heard Paul, why suddenly Paul.

"I don't know. I like Paul."

"Hmm." I think about it. "I have a friend who knows someone named Paul Small. Isn't that a funny name?"

"I like that. Paul Small."

"Should we call you Paul Small?"

"Yeah. Daddy can be Paul Big."

"Or Paul Tall."

Emma says "I wanna be somebody."

"How 'bout you're Molly Small."

"I wanna be Andre."

"ANDRE?"

"Yeah. Emma Andre."

"Okay."

Daddy says "Goodnight Paul Small."

"Goodnight Paul Big."

"Paul Tall."

"Paul Tall."

The next day it's raining. We're outside raking some leaves up off the cement by the pool. Nathan is trying to fix his bike. He's sitting on the tricycle, bundled in his winter clothes, tying some string onto the bike. Mumbling to himself as I pass him. "I'm Paul Wet right now," he says to himself. I start laughing.

Later that day I tell him he's Paul Tired.

Now we're all Paul something. Paul Grumpy. Paul Hungry. Paul Dirty. For three days we're a Paul family. It's like there's never been a time when we weren't a Paul.

Then by the fourth day, he forgets about it. Because once you've been a Nathan for five years, it's hard to remember to be a Paul.

The Cat People

Emma wants a kitty.

The Cat People are at the pet store, with a bunch of kitties in cages, setting up.

Emma crouches down to look in the cages, all stacked up, like they've just been rescued from a flood.

"I like this one," she says, about a four-month-old stripey gray kitty that keeps batting her hand when she pokes her fingers in. He keeps reaching his paw all the way out like those monkeys on <u>Planet of the Apes</u>. No, wait, those monkeys are civilized. Well, whatever.

I go cage to cage looking with a discerning eye at all the choices. I decide all white or all black or orange would be the right one. An old cat, too, not a fresh one.

The cat people keep trying to shoo us away while they set up a little viewing stand for the cats, since they are up for adoption. The cat people are very serious, thin, white-haired women in their seventies who look like they haven't had a decent meal since the Vietnam War. All these boxes of unwanted cats, and women with loose pants looking hungry – add some charcoal, load on the cats and I see an equation for a good meal here.

Emma is now lying on the floor looking mistily in at the stripey baby cat; the two are pledging their love to each other.

The cat ladies won't meet our eyes, they skitter away when you try to touch them. They are, in fact, cats themselves. They set up the wire viewing cages with fresh towels, bowls, food, water, little cat beds, kitty litter, like they're rehousing the homeless.

"Can I hold him? Can I see this one?" Emma is between them, craning her neck up, whining desperately for one of the old ladies to give her a cat to feel.

"Not yet, honey. In a minute, honey." They're doing their set-up ballet. They take the carriers one by one and stick them under the large table, then transfer the cats, one by one into the wire condominium they've built on top of the table, where people can view them. I try to comfort Emma as they take her stripey cat's cage from her grasp and leave us with her heart shredded like a fresh beet. He's only going into another cage, and we watch, patiently, while they futz around until they finally take the kitten out and put him in what they have deemed the appropriate viewing vessel.

He looks the same, just higher up. "Can we see this one?" I ask the less scary of the white-haired women, who has a horsey smile.

"Sure, sit in this chair; you can hold him on your lap."

Emma scurries to sit with me under her, and then they deliver the stripey madhouse right to her arms.

She clutches it by the throat. Her face is rigid in pasted happiness. She's barely breathing.

The kitty purrs and bounces its head against her chin.

He wiggles and climbs up her chest, licks her lip and her cheek and her ear. She loves him but she can't move. She can't express this level of adoration. She's a hard butter stick of love.

"Honey, don't squeeze his neck," I utter the phrase that I know, if we ever got a cat, would become the hourly mantra, along with "don't carry the cat by its head."

I help her to hold it gently around the tummy, and the cat reaches out its front paws across her chest, I fear, to scratch all the varnish off of Emma. Instead, it just lies across her. It can't get anywhere; she has it smashed in her hands like she's wrestling a live snake.

"He likes me. He wants to go home with me." She finally looks up in my direction.

The cat licks my arm. It feels like a friendly razor blade. I scratch his little gray face, and he purrs extra loud. He is really cute. We could keep him outside. We have a barn. The dogs might not eat him.

The daughter of one of the cat rescue ladies, a normal-looking forty-year-old, takes the kitty to put it back.

Emma stands up, breathing for the first time, in a gasp.

I talk to the normal-looking person. "How much is it to adopt one of these guys?" I ask, even though I'm allergic and can't possibly have a cat.

"A hundred dollars."

I could buy a coat made of cats for less money.

"They've had all their shots, been spayed, plus we home deliver them for you, after we do an inspection and we come back two weeks later for a follow up inspection," she rattles off, rationally.

I am not having the cat police visit my house. If I want to get a cat and keep it outside and have it terrorized by my dogs, I'll go to an alley downtown and find my own for free.

Emma pokes at the kitty, her kitty, through his cage. He rubs against her. I rub my face, my runny nose, and feel my eye start to swell up. I might as well have taken the cat and rubbed it all over my face.

"I want to buy a baby kitty," she says.

"But baby kitties grow up to be big kitties," I say.

"But when it gets to be big, I want to put it back," she says.

"Say bye to the kitty, now," I say to Emma, and she looks grateful for this civilized parting.

"Bye," she smiles, longingly, walking away backwards. The cat shoves his leg way out like he's trying to flag down a cab.

I hope he gets his ride out of there – a rich family, no dogs. A place where a hundred dollar cat can really *do* something, like study for a Master's degree.

Emma looks up at me happily. "Let's go see the bunnies now," she says.

Nathan Sleeps with A Severed Arm

Nathan, five, decided he could sleep in his own bed if he had an elbow. Not his own elbow, but a nice squishy elbow like his dad lets him squeeze each night as he falls asleep in our big family bed. We're trying to downsize the bed to Adults Only. This was his helpful suggestion.

We go to the art supply store to find stuff for his birthday cake, and of course we end up sidetracked by glitter and yarn, making our way to the cake section, and then we find the Halloween stuff is out because it's AUGUST, and among them, hanging on the wall, is a bloody, severed arm. Not from one of the employees, a fake one. Nathan grabs the arm, flabbergasted. "MOM! Now I have my own arm. Does it have an elbow??" He searches the torn sleeve with the blood patches on it, and feels for the squish he has come to love since he was nine months old, laying on our arms to go to sleep at night. (Ah, lazy, family bed parenting has kicked our ass – it's five years later and he won't leave the bed.)

He squishes the arm, and can't find an elbow, but I say, in my too-much-time-in-bright-lights-with-no-real-money-to-spend-department-store way, "Well? Do you like it?"

"Definitely. I can sleep if I have this arm!"

We start heading to the checkout counter, while on our way, I start emptying out and ditching all the things that looked good a half hour ago, but that I know I don't need, and leaving them on different racks and stacks of merchandise. I figure it gives the young kid employees something to do when they close and lock the doors and tidy up at night. It's like a treasure hunt for them. They're all an average age of sixteen. They need something useful to do. They don't have that anger about cleaning up that comes about twenty years later when you have two kids.

We get to the checkout and Nathan puts his severed arm up to be scanned. The girl thinks this is funny, that Nathan is so happy about his new arm.

"It's what I've always wanted," he tells her.

He hasn't quite figured out that it's covered in fake blood and looks nasty, to him it's a ticket to peaceful sleep. The elbow represents a very private love affair he's had going for years now.

We get to the car, and I check the receipt, wondering how I spent so much when I only went in for cake decorations, of which I got none, and ended up with ribbons and paint brushes instead. The first item on my receipt is "BLOODY ARM….. $4.99."

I start to laugh. In the parking lot of the multiplex strip mall, Target, Best Buy, Michael's Art Supply, the towering signs pressuring you to buy buy buy, my life circles me and expands out in laughter. My life is a circus. I unlock the car and look at Nathan climbing in, bumping his stiff arm on the car roof. When I was in my teens, planning my wedding to Scott Baio and dreaming of our beautiful kids, I never in a million years pictured this blonde bobbing face getting into my beat up Honda toting his favorite sleep aid, the bloody severed arm. My dreams were so conventional. Lacked daring. I didn't realize then that life could be a) so much harder and b) so much more interesting.

Who says what's important at five years old? A bloody arm for $4.99. I glance at my son in the rear view mirror. The boy is a genius.

We pull out into the stream of Los Angeles traffic, the never ending river of too many cars, too many people, too much shopping. Nathan is inspecting his new rubber hand. "I have to cut his nails," he says, seriously.

(Just for the record, it's been two nights and the arm lies by itself on his bed, while he still crashes with us on the big bed in our room. But we do HAVE the arm, and there will be a time when the arm will have Nathan.)

Santa Can I Have That

Sometime in July I start watching T.V. with Nathan and Emma. We have never watched T.V. with commercials in it, just Disney movies. Not on purpose, just Nathan would never sit through a movie or anything on T.V.; he'd rather be digging something up or playing with a screwdriver. But then Emma came along, a girl who could sit in front of movies all day long, and we start watching movies.

But T.V. introduces us to all these commercials. For the first month when watching a show on T.V. together, every time a commercial would come on, they'd look at me and say "Is it gonna come back on?" They couldn't understand why there were all these interruptions with other stuff that had nothing to do with their show. Then they started watching the commercials. Even on mute, the commercials are always for kids' toys. They wanted everything. I told them "Just ask Santa. He's listening to you all the time. If you see something you like, ask Santa, and he'll remember for you."

It's months later. At every commercial, now, I'll be in the kitchen or the bedroom or the living room, and I'll hear Emma say quietly, "Santa, can I have that?" Or when Nathan's at school, she'll say, "Santa, can Nathan have that?" Then we look through kid toy catalogues we sometimes get in the mail, and they study each toy. "Ohhh!!! Santa can I have that?"

They say it so much every day that I have to say to them "You know, Santa can only bring you one thing." They look at me with horror. I say "He has to take toys to all the kids, everywhere, so he couldn't bring you EVERYTHING. He'll pick something."

This does not stop the requests. They're giving Santa every opportunity.

Now I want something. It's kindergarten's fault. Because Nathan's in kindergarten, and Emma's in preschool for a half-day, it gives me just enough time to realize (three hours, three days a week) that I could be doing something else. And then ziiip – the time is up, gotta go pick up the kids. But that three hours keeps happening, throwing off my Mom Rhythm. I had it down: wake up, do a bunch of stuff for babies all day, nap, do more stuff, go to bed. I'm looking for a new rhythm. Time to add a new baby (every house should have a crib in it); time to add a horse; time to add some more money; a new job; something to fill that void. There's a lot of rushing air, shooting past me, and I don't want to waste any of it, but I can't grab on to anything.

Making the kids was a monumental thing – actually creating a living person out of my papier mache body, and one as pretty much talentless as my body has been. I mean, my body has worked, and delivered me safely to this point in my life, but as far as doing anything extra-curricular, it's pretty much a slacker. I'm not sure how I made people that came out alive and well, and I'm not sure I can follow that up. You can't just follow that up with like, a hat trick.

I have this growing need to create that isn't satisfied by two seven pound balls of children; in fact, it's getting worse, the need – what if it just keeps escalating? Either I have to create something to satisfy the yearning, or I need to carry a gorilla baby. The creating part seems like trying to dam up the Mississippi River with sandbags. The bags keep disappearing into the flowing water. The kids busting out of my body blew a hole in who I thought I was. I don't know the ends of myself. In fact, there might just be a cliff and a great abyss. Maybe a flying car, and Dick Van Dyke in there.

What if life just keeps getting more intense, instead of dulling to the point of oblivion? Then at the end there's just a popping sound and a burst of flames, and then everyone goes out to Sizzler after your memorial?

Forget creating anything. I decide I should just get a horse. We have a barn, there should be a horse. I take my neighbor's horse out to try and kill the urge to buy one. Emma goes on these trail rides with me, often, and chatters away on the front of the horse. We are almost at the mountain, on the path one day, and Emma notices everything. The tunnels animals leave, the way the grass grows, what the dog is doing. She notices a big white X on the ground made of plastic, that I didn't even see.

She says, "You know what that X is for? Treasure."

I laugh and ask her what treasure is.

She says, "You know, necklaces, rings…."

Then as we ride further she says, "Can we dig?" and I say we don't have any shovels, and she says, "We can use our hands."

It isn't the horse. It isn't a new baby. It's Emma, sitting in front of me, in her dancing skirt over striped tights, ballet shoes and velvet purple leotard. Chattering and singing the whole ride. Or being in Nathan's kindergarten, painting. Riding them on the bike, to and from school. Seeing thunderstorms. Brushing their teeth. This is all I get, the only fall season of them being five and three. It's all right in front of me. I want to be present.

Santa, can I have that?

She's Beauty, Now

It's gramma, gramma, the hugeness of my gramma. Getting there – taking the kids on the surreal plane, across the country and then seeing her, in that bed. She doesn't look like gramma; she has no teeth and she's lying down, and she has my gramma's face, or hair, or parts of it, but my gramma never lays down for that long. She isn't ever lying down, she's always at the sink, or making me food, or sitting outside watching us, or laughing at our jokes, or playing cards, or listening to us, or singing, or asking us questions, or doing the jumble in the paper, or watching sports on T.V.. She's busy, busy busy; short and squat like an Indian, but beautiful, her white hair always swept up in a bun. She's solid, effervescent, and yet there she is on the bed. Still.

My mom is playing forties music, because gramma liked old time big band music, and we're in her house, and relatives are coming over, and it's like gramma is just in the bathroom because we're all gathered in gramma's house, but where is *gramma*? The ceramic ducks are up on top of the tub, so I know I am at her house, because the ducks are around the tub watching you take a bath like always, and she has stacks of towels and all her furniture is there and you just want to steal everything, stuff your pockets, take everything because maybe then she won't really be gone.

At night after the kids are asleep I go in and sit with my mom and gramma, and my mom, who has a laundry fetish, is washing maybe one piece of underwear and a pair of socks, just so the laundry will make noise and give her something to keep getting up to do. We're sitting on the bed next to gramma, holding her hand, and the first night she moves a little bit and I can hold her hand and joke with her while she sleeps, and sometimes Mom is laughing, and sometimes Mom is crying and worrying she didn't do enough, she didn't see her enough; but no time would have been enough, even eighty-seven years wasn't enough. And I worry about the kids being this close to death and being afraid of death, but they hug gramma like I do, and I tell them it's good to love people, especially people who have been so good to you. Then I study her fingernails, and I crawl up next to her in bed even though it feels like I'm too old to do that, and I smell her hair and tell her I love her, that she was a great gramma, and she sleeps.

The second night she isn't moving around at all, and her arm is heavy when we lift it, not light like the night before, and my mom who is a death nurse (a convalescent center nurse and knows the stages of death, is in fact, used to death) knows that gramma is heading out, she even helps me understand that spirit is separate from body. And I witness that, I see how different gramma is, as her body stays behind, heavy without the lightness of her energy and spirit. Amazing that the spirit is what makes you light, not heavy;

without the spirit you are just your own flesh, and it's heavy. The spirit is the sponge that squeezes out all your humanity and mortality, day by day; it squeezes out all the excess, trying to make you lighter but in the end you are too heavy. Your body is of this earth, it has to stay, and your spirit has to make the flight alone.

In the middle of all this is me and my mom, and me running in and out, yelling at kids, four and five, too young to understand how to be good for four days straight. We take naps in the closet, on piles of sheets and blankets that gramma hasn't put away. The kids love the closet, make a whole house out of it. They paint watercolors and color pictures, and they smile and make a racket and slide down the stairs, and we take walks to the 7-11 to get Icees, and we go for rides in the minivan. We climb on old piles of snow in the middle of the parking lot at the Safeway since that's the only snow that's left, and I guess this is part of gramma's death too, all this happy life, this vacation for the kids, who only understand that now they suddenly have all these new relatives and lots of attention, followed by huge gaps of time spent without me while I tend to Mom.

In the tub at night I tell the kids about the caterpillars Nathan had in his kindergarten class, and how we watched them go from caterpillars into the chrysalis that was green with gold stripes and after awhile in that chrysalis, a whole other thing came out of it – a butterfly, with wings. I tell them that's sort of what gramma is doing, and it's kind of a miracle. Emma thinks she's going to be a ladybug, not a butterfly.

The night I know she's probably going to die, I go upstairs with the kids and fall asleep with them, knowing I should be down with my mom, but knowing that also I need to sleep with the life around me and that Mom needs to be with her mom.

Mom comes up the stairs early in the morning and I know she's gone, and I get out of the bed and we go downstairs, and it's like a relief because the waiting is over. For a moment we feel good because we're done with one part, and we've done everything right. We call people, and there's a nurse that comes, and a scary funeral guy with a dark blue van and a stretcher and a body bag. I feed the kids breakfast and tell them that gramma is an angel now, and they go into her room and see her, and then they watch her go off in the van. I tell them that gramma could be an angel or a butterfly, and Emma sees a ladybug on the lamp and says, "There's gramma!"

But by that night we're in bad shape. When the kids are asleep I come down to Mom and she's so lost, just wrecked by the death. She and her brother sit at the table reading old letters, and looking bereft. Then everyone's gone, and the hospital bed is empty and I go in to Mom who is lying across the other bed, sideways on her back, holding a clock she must have been setting, but she's asleep because she hasn't been sleeping. So I put her legs on the bed and I take her glasses off, and I scoot her over and I lie next to her. The same way, last night, I came down and found her asleep clutching some cash, next to her mom, money she wanted to give me for something, groceries, but there she was, next to her mom, and now that bed's empty and here I am with my mom, and she's crying and saying you love someone so much and then they die and who's going to talk to her the way gramma did, who's going to be there for her like that, the way your mom is always there for you, the sensible one? I tell her maybe she just has to readjust how she talks and listens to her – she already knows what gramma would say. She just has to look in her own heart and hear her. But my mom's crying so hard, and then I'm crying, and this thing is wiping me out, all this emotion, rivers of it.

Then we're on a plane going home. There's so much stuff to go through at gramma's, but I have to go home. I have to stop yelling at my kids who are small and need me, and deserve their life back. They've been incredibly mature, and they shouldn't be mature, they should be insane. So we're back in our life, and it feels pretend. I feel old and different. I miss my mom, and hope that I don't only feel important when I'm helping somebody. But I feel this gramma time is an epic experience – being so close to the end of someone's life – it makes you extremely vulnerable. Washing my gramma and changing her nightgown, patting her and memorizing her…. It's important to love someone like that. And seeing that we are a body and a spirit, and we are vulnerable to the ones we love at our deaths – we're literally in their hands – she deserved us, and our pampering, in her last moments, whether she was actually aware of it or not. She had us with her. She had my mom, her baby, still there with her, loving her to the last second. I hope I'm this lucky.

I would, of course, tell Emma and Nathan, if this was their scenario with me, that what's more important than my transformation to butterfly at the end is that they love themselves, and not feel so much pain.

It's too big. I did see a butterfly today and realized that it is gramma – she isn't gone – she's just become beauty now. I think of her life lesson, that you can't just blindly love people, you have to see who's worthy of your love before you dish it out, because the love you give out is your only power. You have to believe in yourself and value that love because it is your soul money.

I drag myself to bed. It's good to see Barry, it's been a really long time.

Free Lunch

They're watching me. I'm in the school cafeteria and I just slipped a hamburger into my pocket. They didn't see. Maybe they did. Am I weird? Michelle never eats her lunch. It's a shame to let that lunch go to waste. If I eat her lunch, I don't have to make myself a lunch. This is a big deal. Making the food has me so desperate NOT to make the food, I've resorted to stealing the would-be trash of a five-year-old's lunch. I wouldn't eat food that the kids are GOING to eat. I only eat the food that would be thrown away. Technically, I'm there because I'm volunteering at Nathan's kindergarten, and they always go to lunch at the end of the time I'm volunteering, so I go to help them and just be there. It's on Tuesdays and Thursdays, and Emma is sometimes with me, so she buys a lunch (see, we buy it sometimes), and it's usually disgusting. But really, no, it's not so bad, all the food groups are represented, and while I've never been a fan of a fruit cup, why not eat pre-made lasagna? When's the last time someone made me a warm lasagna and gave it to me in a little tin just for me?? With a spork? And chocolate milk? Michelle sometimes eats her fish fillet, which is a bummer because I'd really like to eat the fish. Usually I'm stuck with the hamburger that tastes like really old shoes.

It's the paranoia that's getting me. In the school newsletter I read something about parents not being allowed to be in the cafeteria when the kids are eating, and I thought, THEY'RE TALKING TO ME. Even though no one's seen me taking the food. But what if the lunch monitors, tough-looking prison guard women, probably in their thirties, that look like they've done some serious time themselves, but are in actuality probably just old hookers, or moms of too many kids, saw me? They would think it was weird that I was so hungry all the time. Hungry enough to eat kids' trash food. I mean most of these people actually cook, and have morals. I just can't stand to see kids throw out buckets of food! The Mom instinct in me just goes rabid. Don't throw that out! If I had big enough pockets (like as long as my pants) I'd just stuff in packet after packet of untouched/unopened (indeed – mint condition) mini-carrots, and then the lasagnas, and the chicken patties, and the nuggets, and the corn dogs, and the spaghetti, and the taco pockets. I wouldn't have to cook for MONTHS.

I try to eat before I go volunteer now – an apple, a carrot – something so I'm not so RAVENOUS while they're all eating. Today was St. Paddy's Day, and it was raining so we ate in the room, and Emma was eating her hot dog, and she didn't like it (not like her, she's the one who introduced ME to corn dogs, a food I had never eaten until her glorious birth and life), so instead of throwing it away, I tasted it and,

Oh my God – possibly the worst hot dog I've ever had in my life. It was actually bitter. I never throw anything out, especially nothing free. Today, for the first time, I threw it out unfinished. In any twelve step program, I know that's progress.

I can't promise that I won't eat the food again. I have made a promise to not eat OTHER children's food, because I could see getting called into the office for a rather embarrassing chat with the principal, where she asks, "Umm… are you EATING the children's food?" instead of the real question, "Why are you so HUNGRY?"

It's because after five years of feeding my babies, all my time is spent FEEDING my babies, and here's this place, this school place, that has all this food, and NO ONE'S EATING IT. Most of it is going into those big black trash cans. I'm a big black trash can. Feed ME. But no, I have to contain myself, even though Michelle never EATS. We've told her mother, but her mother doesn't want to pack her a lunch, so she just sits there drinking her milk and throwing her food away.

I want those ladies in the white hats and plastic gloves to shove crappy food choices at me too. I want them to take my ticket, and yell at me if I take too much ketchup. I want to be taken care of, for free, at least just for one crappy lunch. See, here's my problem: the other lunch monitors either 1. already ate their lunch 2. are getting paid to monitor, not steal food 3. have pride 4. have delicate taste buds. None of these apply to me. I'm just a Freeloader Mom, coming to be with my kid at school so he doesn't forget me, letting my time bleed over into lunch so I can have this combined glorious battle with my kleptomania and Hungry Mom issue.

I was never obsessed with food. Well, chocolate and I go way back. Not an obsession so much as a solid friend. But with all this focus on preparing food, healthy food, balanced food, against-my–better-judgment-food, all these years, I've kicked over the edge. I'm too hungry. It's the truth. Nothing has tasted good since I was single and I didn't have to cook. A meal for me in my twenties was corn. When my kids are grown, my meals will again be corn. It's hard to remember a time when I was just a 'me.' Not a me, with these little mini-mes. Hungry and always needing something. I mean, I'm needy enough just in one complete package. Now I'm the bonus plan.

I wasn't prepared for the actual GROWING of a person. And my cooking skills are so poor. It's Home Ec, all the time. I took Home Ec the same way all the other kids did in Junior High, in order to ignore the teacher holding that paper pyramid up and to daydream about horses. Nobody tells you that this is THE MOST IMPORTANT CLASS YOU'LL EVER TAKE. Forget Chemistry. I've never had to use a Bunson Burner again. But those faux kitchens stocked with real dishes, clean countertops, a colander in each cabinet, and all the menus? How to freeze bread. Plan a week's worth of easy recipes. Those classes around the edges of schools – gym and home ec – the short bus riders of the intellect – of course are all anyone really needs. Stretching and cooking, the only things I really need to use everyday and wish I had studied more. The ones that keep you alive.

So I'm forced to cook while waving a shiny object with my other hand and hope the kids pay more attention to the shiny object than what's in their mouths. I've seen fissures in the lining already. After making stew one day, Nathan sat in the high chair and ate a bite and said, "WHAT IS THIS?!" and I told him, "Crock Pot," and he said, "THIS TASTES LIKE SHIT!" I can see him, hopefully a blossoming chef, becoming fed up with the feeble quality of his meals and starting to cook for us all, before he and his sister's delicate palates are ruined.

Before, being hungry wasn't a curse that meant cooking for four people. It meant getting a burrito, or eating some M&Ms.

I'll be discreet. But for now, I'm grabbing all the free lunch I can.

Silkworms

I've spent the last month going out in the middle of the night to rip off mulberry leaves from our neighbor's tree to feed the plate of white silkworms that are squiggling on Emma's shelf.

The kindergarten gave them to us. They have about four thousand of them, and they tell us that it turns out really cool – the worms get as big as your finger and then go into cocoons and emerge as white butterflies (better known as moths). I don't mind bugs in general. But the silkworms look like – worms. Like the gross worms, worms in dead things. The caterpillars were green, and turned into orange butterflies. Not these.

But we have fourteen of them, and the suckers can eat a MASSIVE amount of leaves. I'm constantly ripping branches off this neighbor's tree – and even though he said I could, when I pull on the branch to bend it to break it (I never bring clippers), a SHOWER of overripe purple mulberries come raining down on me, staining my clothes. I wrestle the branch down, bring it home, tear off the leaves, try to separate the silkworms with their suction cup feet from the dried up mulberry leaves, put them in a little wormy pile, dump off their voluminous black flea egg looking poo, then put down a fresh bed of mulberry leaves, and re-pile the white worms in their new habitat.

As they get bigger, I start to feel some relief that this odyssey is near completion. Excited, even, to see the transformation take place. Our little wormy friends have started one by one to make little white cotton-ball cocoons, and this is exciting. Who knows what will come out?

Then I go into Nathan's kindergarten class to volunteer, and happen to see that many of the school's cocooned silkworms have already emerged. From far away, I just see wings flapping at a fast rate, and I hurry over to see what exactly these little beauties are going to look like after all our hard work.

I stoop down to see the silkworm moths. Oh my God, *they're horrific!* They're like a bad, boxy style of car. The butterfly's slow younger brother. They don't come out looking intelligent and lofty like butterflies. They look bloated and wormy – wings don't improve them – and the worst part is, they flap their wings at high speed, but they can't fly. I ask the teacher, wondering worriedly, can they fly? "Oh no…," she says airily, years of experience dulling the horror. "The Japanese have bred it out of them. All they do is make cocoons. Only the silk is important."

I go into the classroom a week later. The silkworm moths are already dead. Emma is touching the now-petrified bodies, frozen in their non-flight. We nourished these guys, they got huge, made cocoons that looked like cotton balls, stayed inside for awhile, came out, flapped non-stop, never got anywhere, and died on the stick where they emerged. What kind of lesson is this?

I sit next to the tray of dead moths and let the kids read books to me, which is what I am there to do, while Emma paints nearby. I can't stop thinking about the Tray of Death over my shoulder. Even though their lifespan is a mere fraction of mine, I can feel both of us on the same agenda. Flapping really hard and not getting anywhere. Working hard and emerging as something not really much better. Was it better to be the human and KNOW this for a fact? Or to be the moth and just keep pumping mightily, just in case?

I've swallowed the evil I feel this lesson has presented to me. Our silkworms are quietly in their cocoons at home, having not yet emerged. Still incubating. I try not to think about the outcome, but instead be a part of each step in the process. Watching them for a sign of the worms making a hole to get out. Watching them eventually poke their heads out. Seeing their wings dry. Watching them lay eggs and then flap flap flap at high speed. The hole they chew themselves out from is a perfect 'o'. The cocoon is a perfect cylinder, made of pure silk. The glory is in the perfection they make, the fine strands, and not where they're heading. The silkworm has already performed its miracle. It makes silk just from persistently eating a bunch of leaves. It isn't even trying to make silk. It's just eating leaves. For weeks just eating the leaves. Then it weaves what happens to be silk into a bed to rest and change completely into another creature. It's doing exactly what it's supposed to. It isn't trying to get anywhere. At the end it's only flapping its wings because that's what wings are for.

Chain of Fools

We wake up Saturday and I want to go to the snow.

We get on the road to the mountain by ten-thirty. We only have an hour before it's time to get ready for nap. The sky is looking crazy for Los Angeles – dark, leaden clouds, a pirate ship of doom in the sky. Actual hail is coming down through palm trees.

Our car climbs the mountain. There's snow on the side of the road. The kids are excited. Cars passing us going down are covered in snow. The kids shriek. There's a cop up ahead that seems to be stopping cars. Uh oh. Are we smuggling anything? Fruit, or Mexicans? Does anyone care if you smuggle Mexicans anymore? I start to get a bad feeling. Not about Mexicans. I roll down the window. The cop says something about needing chains for the tires. The kids look stricken. He's making the sign with his finger, to turn around. I don't want to turn around. Barry's turning the car around. We're pelted with fear from the backseat. "Aren't we going to the snow? Can't we go sledding?"

Barry points out the sad chainless families playing in the bald patches of snow on the side of the road. Throwing snow balls that look like dandruff. I say. "Let's get chains."

Barry looks at the clock. He hasn't eaten yet today.

"Let's go get a Mexican lunch and then take a nap. Then you can go to that funeral," he says, hopefully. I try to picture my day, all dressed in ski pants with packed food, going back down the mountain, eating one more in a chain of bad burritos, taking screaming kids back home for a nap, then running off for a funeral. My gramma died a few weeks ago. And now a distant friend has died. And our fish died last night. I couldn't do death without snow. Snow first, even if it meant putting off and possibly missing death. "We're getting chains."

The kids yelp in happiness. Barry looks at me, still hungry, but gunning the motor.

Everyone is looking for chains. At the foot of the mountain, hoards of people stuff into Sports Chalet in a disorganized mass. There's a run on chains. A helpless man at the counter tells Barry he'll have to wait at the end of the line and there's no telling if he has the size chains we need.

It's eleven-fifteen. Emma and I have eaten half of our packed food waiting outside of gas stations and tire stores as Barry and Nathan run inside to look for chains. His hands are always empty when they come out. I recently finished reading <u>Moby Dick</u>. I know the folly of chasing something you weren't meant to have. I get on the cell phone.

The Auto Parts Gods guide me to one possible store, in the heart of seedy North Hollywood, where the computer says there is the one set of chains left on Earth that will fit our car. Barry's stomach is eating itself. His eyes are waving a white flag. "If we drive there, even if they have it, we'll have to go all the way back across town, up the mountain –"

"We're getting chains," I say. The kids start hitting each other with My Little Ponies, holding the tails and flinging the hard plastic parts at open eyeballs. It's twelve-fifteen. I would really like to go to that funeral. The guy was a nice guy. I have to make it. But first there must be snow.

We get to the last auto store. We all go in, even though it's hailing, we're in ski clothes, and Emma has bare feet. I scrutinize everyone, assuming they're all here for chains. When it's our turn, the lady goes in the back to look. She comes out with a black bag. I think she's gotten her lunch, but she starts to check us out. Oh, SHE HAS THE CHAINS. This is already ending better then <u>Moby Dick</u>. Barry makes sure they're the right size. Then she rings us up. SIXTY DOLLARS. Barry looks at me, ill. I tell him "Pay up, Daddy. We're going to the snow."

We jam back into the car. Nathan's thrilled with a new bag, and one with actual CHAINS in it. There's a Jack-in-the-Box on the corner. I tell Barry we'll get some food to go, and head directly to snow. In the drive-through, I see Barry lose the will to live. He doesn't want this food. He wants to be lying in a corner somewhere, watching golf. We get possibly the worst lunch of our life, and in protest, Barry pulls over to eat the food slowly by the side of the road. Nathan eats a hamburger over the chain bag, dripping ketchup inside. The kids have now read every book in the car, played with all their toys, eaten everything I brought, even the cookies. They've been in the car for three hours. They're looking to break some skulls.

We go up the mountain again. There's a longer line of cars to the cop this time, but we've got the BAG. We get to the cop. We flash him the bag like it's counterfeit money. We get the nod and the smile. He tells us to put them on if it seems too slippery. We drive gleefully, past all the jammed up cars that are playing in the white parking lot dandruff. Now there's lots of snow, but we need a hill, preferably one that doesn't empty out into the street, that we can sled on. We're on a MOUNTAIN. There aren't any flat parts. We drive farther and farther. No one has chains so there aren't any cars up here. We're alone on the mountain. We finally see the perfect hill. We screech over. This is it.

The kids scramble out of the car. I wrap up their extremities with more material. Nathan left his waterproof gloves at home so of course he has to wear red gardening gloves. We start walking up the hill, I put the blue circle disc sled on the ground, pack Emma on it with me, and we go sliding down, tipping over and falling on our heads halfway down. Nathan goes down, up, down, up, down on his back, down on his face, down with snow shooting up his pants. We make a snowman. Emma finds nuts that look like eyes and we stick them on. She finds a piece of snow that actually looks like a head. We stick that on. We eat snow. We take pictures.

Barry stands at the bottom of the hill looking cold. He looks like he needs something to do. I send him to the car periodically for cameras and gloves. Finally a nasty looking dark silver cloud moves in. A freezing wind starts, blowing ice. "Time to go!" says Barry. We force him to go on one ride on the sled. We drag him up the hill. He gets on the disc with Nathan, I pile on the other one with Emma. They go first, then we go after, and we are going so fast. They are stopped at the bottom of the hill, Barry lying in the snow, and Nathan on his knees, and Nathan looks up, eyes widening as we speed toward him…and SLAM into him, and he flies into the sky and lands like a rocketed cat. He LOVES it. We're all laughing so hard, flat on our backs, real laughter, from the same desperate place that had us scrounging for auto parts, sweeping all that out and coating the place with flowers.

The ice and snow are whipping our faces now, so we hurry to the car. The kids climb in, I get them cups of snow and grape juice from the car, mixing it together to make icees.

"Why's it night outside?" Nathan asks as the dark cloud moves in. Barry snaps into survivor mode. "Let's get the hell out of here."

In moments, the road is covered, there's white everywhere, the windshield is so fogged up that we have to turn the air conditioning on, and even then, Barry and I are slunk way down in our seats to see out the front. Like we could even see the road, which has disappeared anyway. Barry shrieks. "It's been three minutes! What happened!?"

We go about two miles an hour. Our goal now is to NOT HAVE TO USE THE CHAINS. We want to return the chains. We don't want the chains. (Well, Nathan wants the chains. He'd rather have MORE chains.) We drive slowly, so Barry can relive the paralyzing Chicago winters of his youth where a long trip was digging your way to the mailbox.

We get back to the cop, and the road peeks out of the snow. We didn't need our chains. We head past him, ready for civilization. The kids are deep into nap time, and not napping. They've abandoned their grape icees and have delved into tearing up a styrofoam cup and spitting it at each other. Then they practice seeing how hard they can hit each other. We are stopped in traffic for a moment. It seems we can't get down the hill. People are getting out of their cars. OH NO. There's no other way out, this is the only road. I look at the clock. If we can get past this traffic, I can even make it to the funeral on time. The kids are through with the snow. They're tearing up paper towels and rolling it into little balls and sticking them in their noses. They practice howling.

The cars are not moving. A policeman walks by us at the

speed of walking. He disappears around the corner. Forty-five minutes go by. I start having the funeral service in my car. The funeral has begun alright. It's for me. I don't feel like playing 'I Spy' to entertain the kids. I've been entertaining in the car for four hours. I'm all used up. They're four and five, short on sleep and out of ideas too. The only things they can think up at this point involve bursts of screaming and inflicting pain. I start to feel really bad that I'm missing the real funeral. What was I thinking, going to the snow? I should be there for my friend. He was a good guy.

The traffic finally breaks up. We head down the mountain. The kids are tumbling down their slope into Behavior Hell. I tell Barry to drop me off at the cemetery. He tells me I shouldn't go in ski pants. I tell him the guy isn't going to BE there, I don't think he'll mind. Besides, he was a make-up artist for movies. A real hippie. But I decide to listen to Barry on this, because in the end I'm usually glad I did.

We're on the freeway and close to home. Someone's shoe flies by Barry's head. Barry starts yelling at the kids that they're going to be in big trouble when we get home. They never hear him angry, so they laugh 'cause it sounds funny. This infuriates him. We tell the kids their punishment is they have to clean out the car when we get home.

We get home, and Nathan is thrilled with cleaning out the car. He gets two huge bags, one for trash, the other for toys, and starts on his job. He even wants a vacuum. He's never had a better time. I get dressed up and run to the after-funeral party to try and pay some sort of respects to my friend. I get to the house and everyone is dressed like pirates (apparently he was working on <u>Pirates of the Carribbean</u>). I don't know anyone (all my friends went to the service, not the party), so I write my name in a book and, feeling inadequate, I leave. I call my friend Dirk on the way back home and he tells me about the service, and we talk about being left alive, and being taken in the middle of your life, just when things were going well. About how we're not achieving at all what this friend of ours was achieving, and doing so by being kind, and himself, and using his talents.

"He's probably putting make up on God now," I say to Dirk.

He says "No, he's up there, going 'Uhhhh…you don't wanna go with that. Let me fix you up, whole new look.'" Dirk adds, "Hey, where were you?"

"A blizzard," I say.

Back home, kids in bed, Barry puts the chains on my desk to return. I managed to do everything, even though I missed some key parts. I just couldn't face death like that, I'd had so much death recently. I'd rather go on the search for chains, risk the four hours of traffic on the mountain, just for that one sled ride where Nathan went flying and we were all laughing, strewn together. Chain of fools. My friend Richard would have been lying on the snow, laughing with us. I'm sure he was in the sky, looking down while holding the make-up sponge to God's glistening cheek, really study-ing our good time. Shrugging, dabbing his sponge, and saying "It was worth it."

The Cheese Stands Alone

When I was little, children's music wasn't so frightening. I don't remember my mom ever playing me actual children's music. I remember listening to the soundtrack of <u>Peter Pan</u> and <u>Black Beauty</u>, or listening to tapes that read you books out loud as you read along.

Before I had kids, I was a nanny for two families – Taylor's family, and Charlie and Ryan's family. I loved playing with those kids; their houses were neat and beautiful, and the kids were wholly polite and caring. The only time I felt like putting a gun to my temple was when the mom would switch on the <u>Village of the Damned</u> rendering of childhood favorites, "The Wheels on the Bus Go Round and Round" being the least annoying. But something about the perky, upbeat rhythm, the happy, harpy music, the chorus of oversynthesized children's voices, just reached a part of my brain linked to the threat of my own writhing death. That part of my brain I like to keep for myself. A clean part, untouched by bad quality music. This part of my brain has been sullied before, by Barry Manilow and Celine Dion.

Aside from breaking up fights, listening to "Jimmy Crack Corn" for the millionth time is my worst nightmare. My new recent favorite is "The Farmer in the Dell." Who knew how many lyrics this bitch had? It's a song with lyrics that build on each other: the farmer takes the wife, the wife takes the child, the child takes the nurse… and it ends up with possibly the best line in children's music. …The dog takes the cat, the cat takes the rat, the rat takes the cheese…and then "Heigh Ho the derry oh, The Cheese Stands Alone."

The cheese stands alone. And then the song ends. This song mystified me. Does this mean that no one can challenge the cheese? Or does this mean that by the time the songwriters got through the family and the animals and got to the food, they realized they were hungry and said, "Uhhhh…yeah, the cheese doesn't take anybody. The cheese stands alone. Let's go get some burgers." Or is it bigger than that? Are they saying that in the ultimate responsibility game, where everyone "takes" somebody, if you're the cheese, you get off free? I've met many a cheese in my life. I've always been the farmer.

I like to think that the cheese is majestic. The cheese stands alone because it is mighty. It doesn't conform to this cat and mouse game called Life. Or maybe because it has no hands. The cheese can't 'take' anybody because how is cheese going to 'take' anybody? Melt on the floor? The cheese takes the floor? They had to end the song there, because, truly, the cheese does stand alone. The cheese is the end. The cheese is death.

And because the cheese stands righteously alone he is

powerful, while all I do is run around after the wife and the kids and the nurse and the dog and the cat and the rat. The cheese is where we all end up. The cheese is the aged, yet fresh joke at the end. The cheese is us, at rest.

The next time I'm in the car in traffic with two screaming kids in the backseat, and "She'll Be Coming Around the Mountain" is playing, I won't come around the mountain, driving six white horses, up above the world so high, with a knickknack paddywhack, E-I-E-I-O. I'll stop doing. I'll think about the cheese, remember the ending, and embrace the cheese.

The Tooth Fairy is Coming

The Tooth Fairy is coming. I'm so excited, I haven't seen the Tooth Fairy since the '70's. She always came reliably, put a quarter under my pillow on the flat sheet, and took my tooth. Quiet, clean, punctual.

Today after school, after Nathan has burrowed through all the shelves and the fridge in snack frenzy, eating yogurt, fruit nax (as we call fruit snacks), a popsicle, peanuts (I gotta organize a better snack parade), and done his homework, practicing writing the ABC's with capital and small letters, crying when he got to Z because he hasn't done Z yet, and the angle on Z is really hard if you've never done it, and the pencil is really hard to erase when you're five, and you're eating grape jello, and you're tired.

He cries so much I pick him up and pretend he doesn't weigh almost fifty pounds, and carry him over to a chair and sit him on my lap, patting his back like when he was little, and eventually he wears himself down. I bounce him on my knee and he smiles his tiny-toothed smile, his tiny teeth in his handsome, kindergarten face, and we talk about teeth because I notice his two bottom ones, the first two loose renegades, seem especially wiggly. He shows me how they bend over, bowing to the king, and it freaks me out a little, but we finish the homework, then tickle and play slap the hands, and then Punch Each Other.

Emma wakes up and yells "SOMEBODY!" and we go back to the bed and wrestle with her, then we have to go outside because wrestling is turning into kicking in the face, and of course they want to go swimming because it's like eighty degrees in May. We peel back the pool's skin and the kids strip and get in, and I mow the lawn around them and hope they don't drown, then wash the dogs, and then jump in and put the hose in because the pool could use it. Nathan's been begging to have the hose in the pool to play with, and I get about one full minute in the pool before there's a fight over the hose, so I swim over and I'm saying, "Don't rip the hose from someone if you want it, just ask and take turns" as I take the hose (gently for once) from them and Nathan yells "MY TOOTH!" and I see that he had the hose in his mouth, like he was biting a snake in half, and my pulling the hose managed to pull his teeth out.

There's blood and Nathan's saying "THERE'S BLOOD! I BLEEDED!" but the tooth is in his mouth and the other one is holding on to the gums futilely, like trying to swim upstream from Niagra Falls. He rescues the tooth in his mouth and I get it, and we're all excited, and the blood is a little distressing, but I tell Nathan the other tooth is still in there, and he says, *It is?* and reaches up and pulls it right out. Then we're laughing and yelling for Daddy, and I tell him to put the hose in his mouth and spit the water out onto the cement beside the pool. He's dubious, but tries it, keeps trying it. I tell him the cold water will stop the bleeding. He says it doesn't hurt. Emma wants to know when her teeth will come out. She feels hers and says one is loose. She wants to have a celebration too.

The bleeding is subsiding. I'm holding the two teeth in my hand, and now I have a son that looks like a poster for summer childhood – naked, tan, blonde hair surfer length, teeth missing, leaping from the diving board like he's jumping out of a plane. It must be nice to have the freedom to lose body parts and look that beautiful. Every phase of his growing up has been excruciating – only because I didn't want it to go so fast. I didn't want him to start to walk, or start to talk, or go to preschool, or be without me ever...but the teeth thing is so sweet that I like it. I like the little hole in his face; I like this moment, where something surprising happened that changed him, all at once, from someone wonderful into someone more wonderful. I like the new teeth that are showing their little heads. I like everything that comes out of Nathan. He is still so innocent.

They both still get excited when we go to check on the sunflowers that we're growing in the backyard. We had one blossom, and this morning when we go out there are three. And every time I have a heavy box, he says, "Wait, Mom. Lemme get the dolly."

It's like how I felt last Christmas, when they were three and five, and going to bed on Christmas Eve – I was excited because we put out the milk and cookies. The presents were under the tree. The kids were nestled in bed. I thought, *Santa really does come.* Even when you're old. He rides in on that faith, that shiny wonder that they crush into the pillows when we're putting them to sleep. They have me believing – not believing, *knowing.*

When we go out in the morning, I'm as surprised as they are that the morning got here, that Santa came, that we're together, that good things happen all the time.

So I crawl in bed tonight between the greatest things I have going on in my life – the sprawled four-year-old and curled five-year-old, with his new gap in his teeth, and his heart big and beating for all of us, and I think *Yay. The Tooth Fairy is coming.*

I'm Done

"I'M DONE!!"

This is what I hear yelled halfway across the house at least once a day. This means Emma's in the bathroom, and needs a wiping attendant. I don't get there fast enough – in fact, it's not a place I rush to at all. Look at where I'm heading. Instead, I unload the dryer first. Or finish feeding the dog. She knows I'm stalling. She yells again.

"I'm DUUUUUNNNNN!"

If there's some other speedbump in my ultimate path to her bottom, like I'm on the phone and trying to hang up, she waits patiently another moment and then I hear her yell, "SOMEBODY!!!"

This is her second favorite thing to yell. The sliding glass doors in our house are so heavy to open that at just four years old (last month) her tiny bird arms still can't slide them by herself. So if she's outside and I'm inside, or I'm outside and she's inside, she stands at the door yelling "SOMEBODY!!" to let her in. She also yells this when she wakes up from nap and no one's in the bed with her, everyone having fled for more interesting pursuits. I'll be at the computer in "the work" as she calls it, and I'll hear a groggy "Somebody…." From the bedroom. Then louder and louder.

"SummmmmmmmBUDDDDDYYYYY…."

For the second kid, the service is really bad. As the second kid, Emma has learned she has to yell way more. She's a professional, at four. She knows she's got a skill. And she uses it.

At Half-Price Wednesday, Emma and Nathan play on the floor with the toys. A kid older than them (he's maybe six, and an obvious bully) asks Nathan his name. Nathan looks up at him with big flower petal eyes of trust.

"Nathan," he says.

The kid says "That's a baby's name."

Nathan looks shocked. "I'm not a baby," he says softly.

I watch the whole scene from nearby while leafing through the clothes rack of girl's dresses where the top price is $2.99. I won't even pay $2.99 for a dress anymore. $2.99 is a rip off. I've been spoiled by this thrift store, whose prices and quality stock has kept us clothed for the past five years.

Nathan's ambivalent, but Emma is deeply wounded that a bigger boy has said something to hurt her brother. Her mind has fled and she's trying to regroup, gathering her tiny wits to think of something to say back to him. Nathan's just sitting, not sure why the bigger kid is so weird.

The bigger kid swaggers up to the candy machines. Emma raises herself to her towering thirty-six inches, and attacks with her strong voice, which goes hand in hand with her gigantic balls.

"He's not a baby," she says loudly to the bully, walking right at him.

The kid looks like a stunned raccoon. She's shoving her face at him like an angry '50's back-up singer.

"That's my BROTHER. He's not a baby. He's five and I'm four. You can't say that." She doesn't have anything else prepared. The kid is in shock, so she fizzles out, having no more dialogue, so she gestures and mumbles and puts her hand on her hips, and paces back and forth disgustedly, for affect. In her final act, she stalks off and throws him looks, and then she's done, back to regular size and playing.

Most mornings are not complete unless she's dissolved, screaming, into tears at least once before eight a.m., when we have to leave to get Nathan off to school on time. Sometimes it's because she had the wrong cereal. Or her scooter is wet. Usually she's not wearing the shoes she likes, or God forbid I force her to wear overalls.

"I HATE OVERALLS!!" she wails. I realize I never pick out her clothes. She would look weird if I picked out her clothes. Her choices are so much more organic. A fluffy organdy bridesmaid dress with sequins and flowers. A velvet topped black dress with a puffy pink gauze skirt and lace netting and tiny bows. Or her Nancy Reagan red number.

"Put all these hair things in, Mom." She'll even allow me

to rip her hair with the brush if I'll put in a million purple and pink hairpins with glitter on them and set her hair up in a bun "like a ballerina." Then she'll pull on flowered or striped tights, black "dancing shoes" and she's ready. Her clothes never stop her from riding her bike, climbing trees, scraping her stomach, falling, crashing, climbing. She's a busy girl, and dressed to kill.

Partly she's loud because she had to be. As a baby, she learned early that being Number Two means the milk doesn't come as fast, the server is busy with the previous baby (wiping, cleaning or quieting), who came only eighteen months before she showed up. So she persistently yelled, persistently got better service, and decided to keep the yelling; it's served her well. If she were a monkey she'd be throwing fruit at me.

Today she showed me how she could make it the whole way across the monkey bars all by herself.

"How did you learn to do that?" I say, in awe.

"Nathan," she says proudly.

"How did you learn to do that?" I say to Nathan.

"Nobody," he says, proudly.

When I was little I wanted to have a bushel of kids; I wanted loud happy voices, and a loud, happy house, steeped in love. I'm almost forty, my dream may have tapered down to these two little blonde sprites that sleep curled on either side of me at night like love rockets. I thought I'd feel fuller with more kids, but if you take the number you've got and let them fill up your heart with their immense power to make you notice every tiny movement of every piece of the world as it floats gently past them….It's a mountain of children; it's love infinity. Even with only these two. They've ambushed me. Every night before bed in Emma's quiet, slow breathing way, when I close my eyes and pretend I'm sleeping and she pretends to believe me and starts to let herself fall into that sleep chasm, she feels around on my face 'til she finds the corners of my lips, and she turns the corners up until they're smiling. She wants me to go to sleep smiling.

I've put everything off. Let her feel my face – I can only look at her tiny four-year-old fingers for such a short time. Let her yell – there'll be only a few more times she'll yell at me from the bathroom – I don't want it to be over. I know it's coming and I never want to get to that point where

I'm done.

Walking in Puddles

We walk to kindergarten in a thunderstorm. Nathan has pink boots with kitty faces on the toes. Emma has on purple boots.

The school is crowds of kids, a flurry of activity at eight in the morning. We wade into them – the wet raincoats, the one fall tree in California with red leaves in the courtyard – a tiny, spindly maiden aunt of a tree. The sun hiding today, the thunderstorm a miracle in the desert, like the Virgin Mary's face on a grilled cheese sandwich.

We go to the raggedy line lining up for Room 2, and I remember, barely, a time when rooms had such small numbers. Maybe when I started, rooms were just one number, nothing with a "D" or 432 or East. Just Room 2, Mrs. Christopher.

Emma's still in her pajamas, and I hold her at my side even though at three she's thirty pounds and I have the attractive arms of a pro wrestler.

The bell makes a tone sound, three of them, and the teachers come out, release themselves from their classroom gates, and walk up to their lines with off-handed assurance like gladiators to battle.

Nathan, amidst his gaggle of friends, looks up at me, his hand fiddles with my hand. He has a fleeting look of panic.

"I'll walk in there with you," I say around his fear cloud, fluffing it, and smoothing it out.

I think about my grandma, my dad's mom, in the nursing home in South Carolina at ninety. On the phone yesterday, she said breathlessly, in a baby voice, "When I get better I get to go home."

"It's early Alzheimer's," the nurse told us.

We walk in the line to the classroom, and Nathan stops me at intervals to start kissing and hugging.

It's been eleven days since school started. I recognize some of the faces around us – Jorge, with a chipped tooth displayed in a big grin, the twins Norman and Gaby, with matching wire rimmed glasses, the grandfather that drops off Alex, the boy who cried the whole day, the first day. He has a kind face. He watches his kid go with the love attentive on his face, immersed in the sound and the image of the little body in uniform shorts, the way Alex walks away, down the line in the cement like it's a long string out from the grandfather's heart, and he's balancing on it.

I kiss Nathan once more before the heaviness of his class door swings shut, his arms trapped up at his chest like a hermit crab, one hand in a wave with an uncertain look on his face.

I drop Emma at preschool. She usually doesn't care if I leave, but today she says "Mommy, I want you to stay."

She wanders out with me to the door in an echo of

Nathan when he was here, the lone tiny person, in her little purple boots and dress, looking up.

My grandmother isn't much taller than Emma. She had always been picture perfect, a fifties business woman, coiffed, martinis at five. The nurses said on the phone that she was so angry she was having fits – screaming at everyone, hysterical and inconsolable. They had to put her in the clinic.

The first week Nathan was in school the whole family felt seasick. We rode the waves of excitement and hate. His face was hollow that first week of no napping after taking naps every day for five years. Our rhythms in terror mode. The first week of school I sat up late on the internet, trying to find out about homeschooling, seeing if I could justify taking Nathan out of school and keeping him home with me. I'd go to bed frazzled, and say to Barry: "They should tell you you only get them to yourself for four years, then you have to relinquish them to society." He says: "Some things you do because they're good for the child, even if it's bad for you. And socializing is good." For the good of the child?

My grandmother had a nanny raise her child. She kept herself officiously separate. This was, perhaps, the key. Don't get attached; don't feel too much. It's messy, and there's all this pain of letting go.

I infiltrate Nathan's classroom as a volunteer. I disappear into the group, let them surge over me with their five-year-old power of openness. It's like bathing in a volcano, they're so alive. One by one I get to call names as the teacher teaches, and the kids come over to me to paint orange and red and yellow onto paper that will eventually be billowing fall wind socks. She's tricking them into learning colors and counting, while I'm counting the thirteen new children I now have in my imaginary nest. Their big, uncomplicated hearts, like Nathan's, right there on their faces. They're good company. You can be the person you've always wanted to be, your best self. They believe you.

After the painting, the teacher gives me her role sheet to pick names, to take kids on an autumn leaf hunt. As I'm cleaning up paint, I see the role sheet has numbers and grades and I try and see where my son fits in, what's he doing; he's at the top of all the numbers, but most of these kids are just learning English, while already speaking a whole other language fluently, so is he stupid? But then, wait, he's five. I know his heart, and he is well.

I take five kids at a time on the leaf hunt. Nathan looks at me with emergency eyes, praying to get picked for a team where he knows the captain pretty well. I reassure him that he'll get to go the way all the kids get to go, eventually.

Outside the air gasps at us, the rain is cooling or caus-ing the humid air in a desert where we have no rain or humidity. The kids and I are happy to be out like deer in the woods. We look for any yellow or red leaves on the schoolyard trees, and we're new to the schoolyard, so it's an investigation of places none of us have been to. The kids celebrate every dying leaf and blade of grass. They tell me about their brothers and sisters. We dodge puddles and duck under hallway roofs, trying to whisper. We end up in front of the maiden aunt tree, the lone, emaciated tree, with the deepest red leaves shimmering under diamond drops of rain. We all breathe in at once.

The tree looks like it stopped its process toward death to deal us a hand of brilliant colors. There isn't even one to take back with us on the ground, the tree holds them solidly.

The kids and I head back, and I know from Nathan it's not the place you're going or the end result as much as the act of walking and looking. The result is the experience itself, the whispering, the puddles, seeing the color red.

Back in the classroom they're getting ready for lunch. The rest of the kids will have to wait until Thursday when I come back again.

I reunite with my boy to walk in the line to lunch. He has his sweaty, crumpled dollar in his hand. He's buying the chicken patty today, he's a businessman with Spiderman underwear. He looks up at me with big eyes.

"The teacher says walking in puddles on the way to school isn't the best idea. Better to walk in puddles on the way HOME from school."

I look at his wet jeans and agree.

That night, Barry is putting the kids to sleep. I listen to my grandma on the phone. I ask her if she ever walked through puddles while walking my dad to school. I can feel her disintegrating. She made it angrily to ninety and she's scared there, teetering on her perch. To be at the end, and to realize that somehow you missed spending your whole self on somebody important – *It's not anger at all. It's sorrow.*

I go into the bedroom where Barry is lying with the already sleeping Nathan and Emma. I squeeze into a family crack. I can't see Barry but his voice floats over as he recounts bedtime for me, whispering, "Nathan talks and talks and talks. I can tell when he's going. He's so tired. He talks himself out and then he gets real still and he says 'I love you Daddy, I love you Daddy,' and then he's gone."

Epilogue
. . . .

Saving the Best for Last

The whole time I've been pregnant with our third and final child (as my dad keeps insisting, *The last one, right??*) I'm sure I'm faking it. I go into Emma's preschool to pick her up, taking my pregnant stomach with me, and people ask when is the baby coming, how am I feeling, and I just keep thinking, *What if there's nothing in there?* Surely I am faking this one. Is there such a thing as an hysterical pregnancy even when you've seen the ultrasound and found out from the genetic tests that everything's alright?

This third time around, every doctor's appointment I go to I'm sure there'll be something wrong. Every time the doctor hesitates (because she's reading my chart) or turns on the ultrasound to have a look at the floating person in my pelvis, I cringe inwardly. *Please let it all be okay.*

Over a year ago I had a miscarriage at twelve weeks. This was the last time I had a person occupying my lower regions. My doctor, whom I had always loved, turned on the ultrasound hoping for the best. I'd been bleeding for a whole day. I started bleeding at Open House at Nathan's school, at his kindergarten class. I could feel the baby slipping out. The doctor said you can bleed a lot and the baby is still in there, still fine. She seemed so positive. Then she turned on the ultrasound and there was the baby in there. My doctor was quiet a long moment, searching, the plastic wand on my gooey stomach inching around. The quiet got quieter. There was a baby but there was no movement. It was a shadow baby. Just a picture on the screen. "I'm sorry," she said, "There's no heartbeat."

Sitting in her office, which I guess is the procedure for miscarriage, she looked at me. I felt like I was in a movie – this was the tragedy part. She was telling me my options. I could just let it continue to bleed out or I could have a D and C. *Are you sure there's no heartbeat?* I wanted to say. *This can't be true, and what if we made a mistake? What if it's alive but we took it out by mistake?* I stared at her leather sofa with the hard silver buttons. She would have the D and C, because it's over with faster, she said.

I left the parking garage and called Barry. "The baby's dead," I said, in the dark garage, looking out into the blinding Santa Monica sunshine after paying eight bucks for twenty minutes of horrendous news. I couldn't feel anything. I was walled off. He was in San Diego shooting something, working. I heard his voice crack.

"What?" he said. His voice had all the pain. He had all our anguish. In him were all the feelings I couldn't use right then or I'd still be in the parking garage, years later, broken. He couldn't leave work. He was stuck there. I told him there was nothing he could do, it was all done, I just had to have the procedure done and it was all matter of fact; the baby wasn't there anymore.

I spent the next few hours on blinding white freeways, going home and then back to the doctor. Paying money to have a procedure I didn't want. My mom went with me. When I got to the clinic and they gave me a gown, I went into the room to change, that's when I started shaking and crying. There was really no baby in there anymore. This was really over.

My mom sat with me until they took me away. I don't remember the room they took me to. I remember coming home and going to bed.

Barry was supposed to go to Arizona for work. It was two days later. I didn't want him to be away. We were eating at a rib place in Los Feliz – Oscar's – and the kids were wiggling around us covered in barbeque sauce. He was supposed to leave tomorrow. Don't go, I said. We called the airlines and paid an incredible amount of money to go with him, all of us. What's nine hundred dollars, he said.

In Arizona we were out in the minimalist desert, at a deserted dude ranch where the huge empty kitchen was darkly lit at night like in a horror film. They were shooting extreme sports – motocross – building a huge mound of dirt out by the horse corrals for the motorcycles to jump. The cameraman's wife brought her new baby to the long breakfast table in the lodge. I looked at this white, bubbling baby, and I love babies, but this one I couldn't feel.

We took our picture on a lone stretch of abandoned highway with the red cliffs of the desert behind us. We clutched our two gorgeous, strapping babies. Later, watching our kids play and thinking about our lost baby, Barry told me quietly, "It's amazing how attached you get to something you can't see or touch."

A year and a half later I tell Barry from the bathtub that I'm pregnant. I worked hard to get pregnant again, not expecting it to work. And now during the whole pregnancy I'm sure it won't stick. Because of the last time.

The doctor is going to induce me because he's going away on the day we're due. Things have changed; we don't have money this time around, so we have cheap insurance and this (luckily nice) new doctor. We get to the hospital and I still don't believe my pregnant reflection in the window, or in the elevator door. We get to the room and they strap on the monitors. This is where last time, with Emma, it was fun. I was excited because the baby was coming. Last time I didn't think for a minute that she wouldn't be perfect. This one, I know that things can go wrong. I am expecting wrong. Hoping for right.

I make it from two to four centimeters before I need the epidural. Then an hour later it's time to push. At forty, the pushing seems harder, I seem not as good at it as I was five years ago with Emma. I'm not having pain, but I'm having to really push hard and it doesn't seem like anything is happening, although everyone around me seems very excited. Everything feels like it's happening in slow motion, the doctor performing some kind of experiment down there in his gown, with instruments and oils and buckets. Each minute seems to be taking hours.

Then there she is. First her head. Then her ear. Then her shoulder. Then it's a her. We didn't know ahead of time. We thought it'd be a Will. Turns out to be a Lilly.

Lilly! There is a person in there. And she has no teeth. She seems to be all in one piece. She is crying hard.

They clean her up; they bring her back over lay her on me. I can't remember this part. She's alive and well. She's here. The family is celebrating, the brothers and sister come in to meet her, the grandparents are thrilled, everyone comes to see. She nurses right away. Later everyone leaves to go see her get her bath, and my niece, Neisha, stays because someone should stay with the mom.

She's here, and she's alive.

I remember staying in the hospital with my first baby, Nathan, and how it was like winning a free vacation. Food and rest, and a brand new baby, the ultimate vacation. With the second baby, Emma, eighteen months later, it was less of a vacation because I wanted to get home to my first baby.

And now here's Lilly Bessie. Five years after that. I don't remember bleeding quite so much, or barely being able to walk to the bathroom. It looks like a vampire movie, there's so much blood. But we are alone in the room and there is this silent beautiful baby in my bed, and all this activity, all these friends and family that we have built, and that have built up around us these past seven years since we had Nathan. Nathan was born into the calm eye of the storm. Emma was coughed out ten minutes later. Lilly Bess was born into a whirlwind.

I lie there awake when the clock makes no sense, seeing every hour like we're old friends, Oh look, this is what it looks like at three a.m., a lot like it looks like at eleven p.m. or four a.m. There's this person next to me in the bed that made it out; the card says "I'm a Girl!" I don't keep her in that plastic bassinet, I keep her in the bed because how can she be here? I'm not letting go of her. I tell her, in case she's actually real, that she's got the most amazing daddy in the whole world. And she has a great sister and brothers. And that we waited for her to come.

My neighbor Junie told me after the miscarriage that the soul of the baby who died just wasn't ready to be out in the world yet. The next baby, she told me, will be double-souled since the first soul was stacked up in there ready to be used. She'll be special.

We gave Lilly her middle name Bessie for my great-grandmother Bessie Haley, who had fifteen children back in the day when fifteen children was like having two. My gramma, her daughter, always told me stories about her family, growing up with that many kids, and it always sounded like so much fun, to have all that company. All those kids, all that energy, all those hopeful faces.

It's amazing how attached you get to something you can't see or touch.

And now here she is, three months later, and the kids hug and kiss her all over, she belongs more to all of us than to me, she's like a great delicious love pie that I brought home that nobody can quite finish. I can barely get a moment in with her. Nathan and Emma anxiously wait for their time to hold her, to burp her, to kiss her, to breathe on her. I don't know if it's me, or if there's just so much more life in the way with the third baby, she's simultaneously always going to be running to catch up and being carried half the way by some loving arm. She's a gentle and patient baby. She is entertained merely by being awake and seeing all the faces vying for her attention. Maybe she sees from inside a head crowded with fifteen old souls, all of whom have celebrated our family before, in earlier installations. Maybe they're pointing out all the wonderful parts of life from her blue glass windowpane eyes, and propelling her big genuine smiles.

I haven't had my real turn with her yet; she's still the phantom baby, baby #3. I'm pretty sure she's really here because she's growing, and the kids see her, and she's started talking loudly to us in the pool. Loud conversations of nonsense. Well, of babysense. I know she's here because there are diapers again, and we have to buy a bigger car, to fit all of us.

I'd love to have more kids, keep creating kids, be immersed in the mystery of the whole process, and the glacier of love that hits your house afterwards and forever. But I look at Lilly Bessie, and I know I'm getting old, that this is it, this little shiny face that survived the re-entry heat, who grows sturdy. I'm not sorry for the end of the process — there's a lot ahead, steering and balancing, and squeezing out bad influences, and shaping a nice big doughy heart for her to bake later throughout her adulthood. It feels like nature puts a cap on your fertility because otherwise there would be no end to leaping into the infinite process that is baby-making, and being washed up on its profound shores. Plus houses aren't big enough. Perhaps if we started our own village.

Like the original Bess, who was the start of this whole mess by cranking out fifteen glorious children in the early nineteen-hundreds. Maybe there is no ending, now that our Lilly Bess is amongst us, radiating her gentle beauty on us mere mortals, here to entertain and enlighten us until she can toddle off and later walk gracefully away, into her own life. Unknowingly, she will be the start of some other, future great-granddaughter's life story. Maybe we thought we were trying so hard, saving our Bess for last, and here she is just the start.

About the Author

Juliet Johnson's plays have been produced at *Mobtown Players, SoHo Repertory, The Samuel French One-Act Play Festival,* and *Coffeehouse Theater,* among others. Her non-fiction has been published in *Los Angeles Family, Mamazine, MOMbo* and *The Imperfect Parent,* as well as in two anthologies. An NYU grad, she grew up traipsing around the back lot of Universal Studios with her brothers while her dad made television shows. Working on movies and T.V. made her think that dreams were possible, and that you could get paid a lot of money for standing around in your shorts. She lives in Los Angeles with her husband Barry (met on a horror film), kids Nathan, Emma, baby Lilly, sometimes big brother Bruce, and Gramma Moose. She drives for a horse-drawn carriage company.

http://www.somebodysalwayshungry.com/

Wyatt-MacKenzie Publishing, Inc.
DEADWOOD, OREGON
www.wymacpublishing.com

Printed in the United States
131133LV00005B/64/P